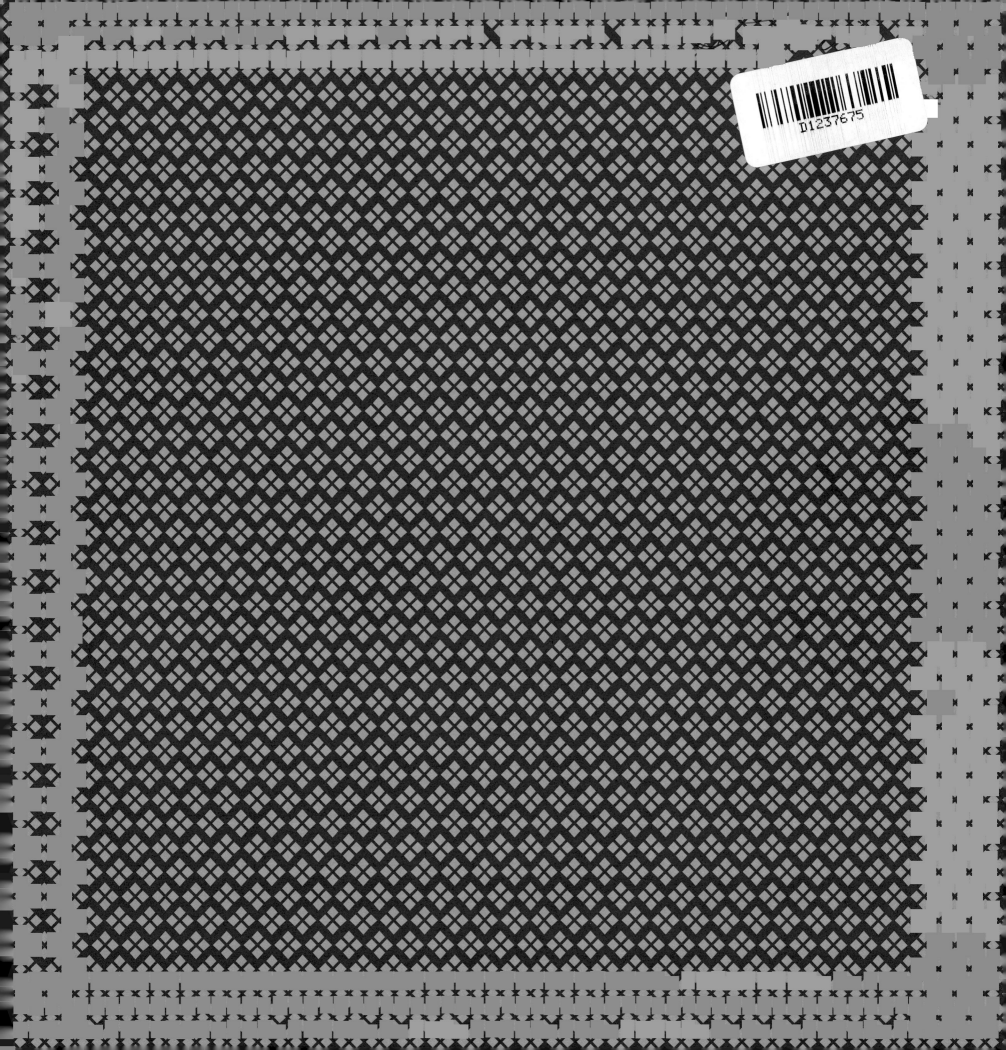

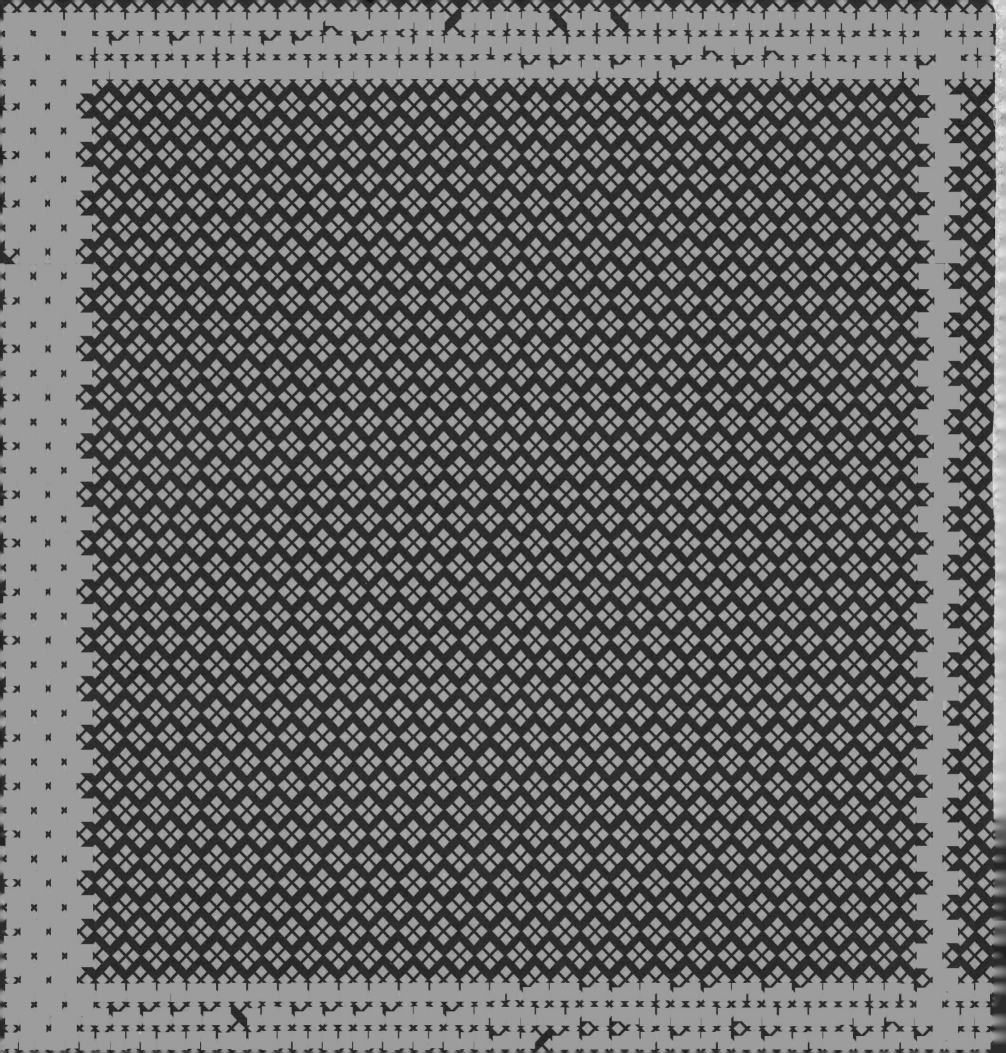

A BENEDICTION OF PLACE

HISTORIC CATHOLIC SACRED SITES

OF KENTUCKY

AND SOUTHERN INDIANA

Our Lady Of The Woods Chapel is one of the most recent sanctuaries to be dedicated
in the Louisville area. Blending modern and medieval elements in its design,
the chapel opened in May, 2001.

❖❖❖

*Proceeds from the sale of this book will go to support the ongoing service of
Our Lady Of The Woods Chapel to the Bellarmine Community.*

A BENEDICTION OF PLACE

HISTORIC CATHOLIC SACRED SITES

OF KENTUCKY

AND SOUTHERN INDIANA

CLYDE F. CREWS

BELLARMINE UNIVERSITY

2002

COPYRIGHT © 2002

CLYDE F. CREWS

ISBN #0-9638927-3-8

BOOK DESIGN

KEN BICKEL GRAPHICS

SPECIAL GUEST PHOTOGRAPHERS

DAN DRY

—

JOHN NATION

—

PATRICK L. PFISTER

BELLARMINE UNIVERSITY PRESS • LOUISVILLE • 2002

PRINTED BY CARDINAL PRINTING

TABLE OF CONTENTS

...for my house will be called a house of prayer for all the peoples.

The Jerusalem Bible
Isaiah 56:7
Mark 11:17

DEDICATION

TO THOSE WHO PERISHED IN TERRORIST ATTACKS IN THE UNITED STATES ON

SEPTEMBER 11, 2001 — AND TO THOSE WHO SERVED IN RESCUE AND RELIEF.

MAY THEY ALL ATTAIN THE DIVINE BENEDICTION AND PLACES OF ULTIMATE PEACE.

FOREWORD

BY DR. THOMAS D. CLARK

Within the scope of two-and-a-half centuries of Euro-Anglo occupation of the North American continent a phenomenal number of historical landmarks have been plastered on the land. Nowhere is this more true than in the Kentucky-Indiana region. Here are the spots where state governments were formed, counties were created amidst public squares, and cross roads were knitted into main streets of towns and villages. All of these in their own particular way give evidence of the spread of American civilization.

To individuals of each succeeding generation these landmarks embody the very essence of place and the passage of time. They embody the inner spiritual attachments to land and history. The monuments of specific times and places document as clearly as any record can, a sense of history. They reveal aspirations of some form of perpetual memory as any human record can achieve.

Perhaps no monumental landmarks in the history of a locality demonstrate more clearly the hopes and aspirations of a people than the church houses, both Catholic and Protestant. None reflect more clearly a sense of history, of contemporary forms, and of the state of the arts. There are the gothic, baroque, plain colonial and rural style houses, all of them expressing the faiths and cultural aspiration of their doctrinal persuasions.

Beyond the religious and architectural elements, the church house, yard, and adjoining cemeteries represent a vital social and politically centralizing force in American folk history. The church house and cemetery have ever been revered places. For instance, cemeteries are really extensions of communities into the past, but they also have implications for the future of generations yet to come.

Tragically the shifting sands of change have left many churches abandoned because of the social and economic shifts within communities and individual human lives. The changes have often left cemeteries and church house sites to the mercies of nature itself. Nevertheless monumental tomb markers have survived with legible inscriptions bearing rich historical data. Even more, grave markers reflect changes in artistic designs; their inscriptions reveal changes in taste and the depth of emotions of passing generations.

This book's text and illustrations reflect the deep spiritual meaning of the churches and their associated landmarks in the lives of their human flocks. In many instances the Catholic church edifices reflect in material and architectural forms the devotion of early congregations. Of equal importance, the church houses and their associated structures actually stand as landmarks along the paths of expansion and within the process of pioneering in the sprawling lands of the republic. For instance the two waves of Catholic emigration onto the Kentucky-Ohio Valley frontier have rich and colorful individualistic histories. The migration of the Marylanders onto the Kentucky central western frontier had a distinctive bearing on local history. In the mid-nineteenth century immigration hub, Louisville, there occurred the "Bloody Monday" nativistic tragedy which has ever been a blot on Kentucky's past. This was an occasion when both the social and democratic political systems ran awry.

In an earlier book, *The Faithful Image*, Clyde Crews created a graphic documentary of Catholic personalities, landmarks, and historical experiences. A distinctive segment of his new book, *A Benediction Of Place*, deals with the blending of personal and institutional life dating far back into the past. Down through the unfolding times social and cultural advancements have been the most reliable gauges of man's civilizing advancements. This book, defining the historical advancement of a religious body, sets an example which all organized faiths should follow.

Hendrick Van Somer.
Saint Jerome in the Wilderness, 1651.
Collection of The Speed Art Museum,
Louisville, Kentucky.

ACKNOWLEDGMENTS

If someone hasn't already said it, someone ought to say it — if you want to see how inter-connected we all are, how truly dependent on one another: write a book. So it truly is that this volume has come into existence because of the professional competence and kindnesses of quite a number of individuals. They will always have my great gratitude.

In the world of archives and historical centers, I begin with that of the Archdiocese of Louisville and Chancellor and archivist Fr. Dale Cieslik, a tireless, resourceful helper. At the Archives of the Archdiocese of Indianapolis, my appreciation to Ms. Janet Newland and Fr. Jack Porter; to Mr. Tom Ward in the Diocese of Covington; to Mr. Jim Paris at the Diocese of Lexington; to Sister Emma Cecilia Busam, O.S.U. and Fr. Pat Reynolds at the Diocese of Owensboro; to Fr. Gregory Chamberlin, O.S.B., at the Cathedral in Evansville; to Mr. Joe Duerr, editor of **The Record**; to Mr. Kenny Popp and Mr. Bill Schreiber at Catholic Cemeteries Office in Louisville.

Without the remarkable archival centers of the religious communities in this region, this book could scarcely have come into being. I salute these leaders who devote so much passion and professionalism to maintaining our collective past as prologue to our future: to Jonathan Montaldo at Bellarmine University; Brother Patrick Hart O.C.S.O. at the Abbey of Gethsemani; to Sisters Katherine Misbauer S.L. and Mary Swain S.L. at the Motherhouse of the Sisters of Loretto; to Fr. Cyprian Davis O.S.B. at the Archabbey of St. Meinrad; to Sisters Bridgid Clifford S.C.N., Frances Krumpelman S.C.N., and Irene Satory S.C.N. at the Motherhouse of the Sisters of Charity of Nazareth; to

Sister Mary Imogine Perrin S.C.N. at Spalding University; to Sister Louise Quinlan, O.P. Springfield; to Sister Martha Jacob O.S.U. at the Motherhouse of the Ursuline Sisters in Louisville; to Sister Emma Cecilia Busam at the Motherhouse of the Ursuline Sisters at Maple Mount; to Sister Eileen Ann Kelly, S.P., of the Sisters of Providence; and to Ms. Flaget Nally at Spalding Hall in Bardstown. To Fr. Sean Hoppe, O.S.B. at Leopold, Indiana; Mr. Robert Harpenau at Troy, Indiana; Mr. Thom Whittinghill at Louisville's Cathedral Heritage Foundation; and Mr. Paul Leingang at **The Message**, in Evansville.

I am especially indebted to Dr. Joseph White both for his personal suggestions as well as his splendid book (cited in the bibliography) on significant religious sites of Indiana. And to Dr. Thomas D. Clark, our Kentucky historian supreme for his thoughtful questions and gracious foreword. At the Kentucky Division of the downtown Louisville Free Public Library, I have often welcomed the help of that stalwart group of pros: Yudora S. Brown, Janie Davis, Melinda Feldman, Joe Hardesty, Lois Tucker and Sue Ann Wight. In the world of the Arts, I deeply appreciate the assistance of Ms. Mary Bryan Hood, Director of the Owensboro Museum of Art; and of Ms. Lisa Parrott Rolfe and Dr. Roy Fuller at the Speed Museum of Art in Louisville. And we are all indebted to professional photographers who have joined heart and soul and skill in producing some of the truly striking images in this collection.

Coming closer to home, as always I am grateful to Archbishop Thomas Kelly for his hearty encouragement. At Bellarmine

University, to President Jay McGowan who urged this project on me; to Ms. Joan Riggert, Ms. Lucy Burns and Ms. Kelly Hickman for their assistance; to my mother Nell Crews for her typing help on yet another of her son's madcap publishing ventures; to Mr. Steve Crews and Ms. Debbie Shannon for editorial assistance. I want specially to thank and celebrate the extraordinary graphic skill, insight and expertise of my friend and designer Mr. Ken Bickel. Most especially I wish to thank Joyce and Damian Alagia. It was Joyce who conceived the idea of such a work and remained its driving force, insisting that prayers and dreams **can** come true.

I would like to note and acknowledge that throughout this book I have included specific dates and the names of architects in some cases but not others. I shamelessly admit that because of the nature of this work — it is a book of experiences, images and impressions rather than of scholarship — I have put such specifics in usually when it was of easy access in my work and travels.

Finally, I would like to acknowledge my own humility that deepened with this work. I began this work thinking that I knew a good deal about the Catholic history of this area. I learned ever so much new in this pursuit and realize how much I have yet to learn about these lands exquisitely rich in their history. It remains my deep hope that others will pursue these studies much further, both in Catholicism and in the many other religious traditions that share this fabled region with us.

Please see also additional listing in Photographic Sources at the back of this book. May 26, 2001

St. Joseph Church in the Butchertown section of Louisville.

INTRODUCTION

A BENEDICTION OF PLACE

I. Sacred Places - Far and Wide

"I think God has given us the love of special places ... for a good reason ... I mean that God bade me love one spot and serve it, and do all things however wild in praise of it, so that this one spot might be a witness against all the infinities and the sophistries, that Paradise is somewhere and not [just] anywhere, is something and not [just] anything."

G. K. Chesterton, **Manalive**

The pages that follow seek to portray a selective visual tour of many of the sites sacred to Catholics in Kentucky and southern Indiana. Such sacred places form part of a network, as it were, of countless sites of intensity and solemnity around the world.

Place here, of course, means far more than an area measured by meter sticks or surveyor's tools. It is decidedly more than a territory described by square footage or mileage. We mean by place something more akin to that which has been enunciated by such phenomenologists of religion as Mircea Eliade or Joseph Campbell: a sacred precinct that casts or conveys a radiance of meaning and power on a people. We are speaking of place as definitional, hallowing, sacramental or transformative.[1]

Sacred space in Eliade does not cast off into insignificance the vast amount of other places in a land or continent. Rather it does precisely the opposite: it gathers up and concentrates significance so that all other space takes on new meaning in its luster. This may sound to persons hearing it for the first time extravagant, overheated or, pardon the expression, spacey. But the persistence and power of sacred place is attested over and over again in our anthropology, our history and our language.

Eliade concentrates frequently on the mountain as sacred space, the meeting point of heaven and earth. For vast numbers of primitive or pre-literate people, the mountain is a mighty place that connects ordinary people who touch it to cosmic cycles, rhythms and patterns much vaster and powerful than themselves alone. The story of sacred spaces does not cease, of course, with preliterate cultures. Consider: Mount Sinai or Mount Horeb (place of the Burning Bush) in Judaism; Mount Tabor, The Mount of Olives or The Sermon on the Mount in Christianity; The Kaaba and the Dome of the Rock in Islam. Every altar in a Christian church takes its name from the Latin word *altus*, meaning high.

The oldest surviving epic, **Gilgamesh**, composed some 5,000 years ago in Sumeria, recounts the story of a sacred grove of cedar trees. The Roman poet Ovid speaks of a "solid grove black with the shade of oak," in which the visitor might well exclaim, "There is a spirit here."[2] Aztec mythological chronicles report that "the first thing the Aztec did in their new city was to establish its center in order to distinguish sacred from profane space. It was important for them to affirm the center of Aztec social space and the cosmological center of the earth."[3]

But the power of place is hardly limited to the ancient and classical past. As J. Donald Hughes has written:

"That is really what we are challenged to do today: to find the places where we connect with the larger cosmos; to keep them free of the impedimenta that would block access to the spirit; and to open ourselves to the values that come from those places."[4]

The siren call to visit such sacred environments is more insistently being heard across this American land. Our people are increasingly traveling to (and reading guidebooks about) hallowed places of nature across the national landscape. Something of the majesty of nature was already clearly a driving force when Theodore Roosevelt began the movement toward national park lands. But now we find deepening interest in places of smaller and intense scale: Mystery Hill, New Hampshire (called America's Stonehenge); Serpent Mound in Ohio; Cahokia Mounds in Illinois; Poverty Point, Louisiana; Bear Butte, South Dakota; Mesa Verde, Colorado; Canon de Chelly, Arizona.[5]

Was not Martin Luther King, Jr., alive and alert to such a sensibility in his epochal March on Washington ("I Have A Dream") Address?

From the prodigious hilltops of New Hampshire...
From the mighty mountains of New York...
From the snow-capped Rockies of Colorado...
From Stone Mountain of Georgia...
From every hill and molehill of Mississippi...
From every mountainside, let freedom ring.[6]

Do you think this came from a man who did not understand the symbolic power of the mountain and its uniqueness from place to place?

Even in places that many of us may have

written off as barren and lifeless, power and life are being re-asserted by their residents and writers. Kathleen Norris writes in **Dakota: A Spiritual Geography:**

"The land and sky of the West often fill what Thoreau termed our 'need to witness our limits transgressed.' "[7]

The tide and temperature are clearly rising in American thought concerning such a variety of sacred sites. Such heightened interest can be explained in part by newer sensibility to Native American culture and perhaps to some smaller degree by New Age sensibilities as well. But the increasing attention to sacred places has entered more into the intellectual mainstream as well. In fact, with either apologies or plaudits to William James who started off the twentieth century with **The Varieties of Religious Experience**, we may anticipate some religious genius of this new century producing The Varieties of Religious Location.

In recent years, the **New York Times Book Review** has favorably, and almost reverently, considered such works as Kathleen Norris's **Dakota: A Spiritual Geography**; Diana Kappel-Smith's **Desert Time: A Journey Through the American Southwest**; and James S. Griffith's **Beliefs and Holy Places**.[8] Just as telling, when the Art Institute of Chicago mounted a major exhibition to note the 500th anniversary of European involvement in the Western Hemisphere in 1992, its title and theme was: The Ancient Americas: Art from Sacred Landscapes. More recently, Margaret Visser's **The Geometry of Love** has shown the power of sacred place —"an ordinary church"— to educate and elucidate as well as edify.

Sacred places have ever exerted an immensely powerful pull on humanity whether they be considered emotionally, psychologically, sociologically, or spiritually. They can transform a peripheral and scattered people into a centered one. They can aid the process that leads a drifting community into a directional one. We shape places, but more profoundly, they shape us. We interact with places in our quests for security, identity and significance.

This nation has become increasingly mobile, modular, urbanized, suburbanized, exurbanized, uprooted, generic, mall-oriented. It also has become, by no amazing accident, more hungry for stability points, mooring places and roots. Or to cite Robert Bellah's **Habits of the Heart**, it is a nation that craves continuity, coherence and community.[9]

One of the many ways that religions in America can serve this nation well is to help it to discover and satisfy this craving. No small part of this task is for the faiths to re-discover and celebrate many of the sites that render them rooted, primal and significant. By seeking out their own sacred places and drawing nurture from them, by learning again from the sacred places their own special gifts and emphases to bring to the American tapestry, the major American faiths are more keenly poised for renewal and service. They find a form of salvation here; an escape from pallid, ineffectual religious uniformity. They

are spared the ignominy of becoming metaphysically identical malls on the nation's spiritual landscape.

II. Sacred Places - Close to Home: Kentucky and Southern Indiana

Kentucky and its neighbor southern Indiana are blessed with a galaxy of hallowed and defining places. The lands all around us are rich in the wonders of nature: knobs and mountains, lakes and rivers, caves and caverns, falls and fossils, verdant flatlands and rolling bluegrass. Down river from Louisville, Angel and Wickliffe Mounds remind us of once-flourishing Native American spirituality. In Louisville, The Gardens at Sixth and Muhammad Ali Boulevard, and the land just to the east of the Kentucky Center for the Arts at Fifth and Main Streets, are the sites of early Indian mounds as well.

In addition to many old churches and cathedrals, synagogues and temples, newer Buddhist, Hindu and Islamic centers, the Presbyterian and Baptist Seminaries, Louisville is ringed round with sites of deep religious history that continue to nurture and shape and define us: Shaker villages at Pleasant Hill and South Union; Cane Ridge in Bourbon County, the focus of Protestant America's "Second Great Awakening" in 1801; Asbury and Lexington Seminaries in the Bluegrass - to name but a few.

Kentucky and southern Indiana have a considerable range of valued and varied traditions of faith. We plan to focus in this book - mostly visually - on one of the more remarkable religious stories of this two state region - that of Roman Catholics in these climes from their foundations in the eighteenth century until about the time, more or less, of the First World War. Thus, our scope has to be selective, representational and limited. We know that others have told - and in the future will tell even more - of the striking lore of our neighboring traditions of faith.

The photos that follow from the Commonwealth of Kentucky are drawn from sites and archives in the Archdiocese of Louisville as well as the Dioceses of Covington, Owensboro and Lexington. In Indiana, we have ventured through southern parts of the state, drawing from the lower reaches of the Archdiocese of Indianapolis (south of the capital city) and the Diocese of Evansville. While the geographical range is extensive, the starting point and central focus is the Louisville area and nearby "Kentucky Holy Land".

These areas comprise some of the more storied lands of Catholicism in America. The narrative will flow in various ways through the chapters that follow. But suffice it to say that Kentucky in the late eighteenth and early nineteenth centuries was to become America's first inland diocese. Its laity came of mostly British-Maryland stock, with a few African and other ethnic people as well. The clerical leaders were mainly French and helped to create in Kentucky's "Holy Land" (see page 68) a source of piety, energy and leadership that would help to establish Catholicism throughout the Midwest and Upper South. The native sisterhoods of resourceful women formed here would be among the very first in the new American nation. To this day the region has an enormous

heritage that remains from those years of motherhouses, academies, colleges and other institutions that began in that era. In Kentucky Catholicism, the first congregations were formed by the laity; the first seminary began on a flatboat; one of the first colleges began life in an old distillery. This will be, in truth, a distinctive and inviting place.

In Indiana, the roots and results are also amazing. The first congregation there - in Vincennes - was predominantly French, though the inflow of Germans in the early nineteenth century (as in parts of Kentucky as well) would shift the ethnic balance. The first bishop of Indiana, Simon Bruté, had been a physician before becoming a priest. The second bishop, Celestine de la Hailandière, had been an attorney. The "Holy Hills" of Indiana, as well as its broad plains, bear witness today to a vast network of convents, monasteries, parishes and institutions of faith. Many will be be seen in the pages that follow.

Our presentation aims to be iconic and impressionistic. That is to say, it does not set out to tell a comprehensive story. A selective and brief bibliography at this book's end will offer the reader several additional resources. Not every site of beauty and significance can possibly be included. Far from it. But we hope that enough appear in these pages to make lasting impressions of the impact of faith on our urban and rural landscapes. We hope too that the contents here will remind readers of the many faithful who have gone before us in these places, all of them bearers of grace and mystery. Seeing these people and places, may we remember, preserve and celebrate. And may we be made aware once again that the seemingly ordinary places of

our lives may not be so ordinary after all - they may be places of renewed insight, energy and benediction.

NOTES

[1] See Mircea Eliade, **Cosmos and History** (New York: Harper, 1959) and **A History of Religious Ideas** (3 vols.) (Chicago: University of Chicago Press, 1978). Also see Joseph Campbell, **The Masks of God** (4 vols.) (New York: Viking Press, 1974).

[2] J. Donald Hughes, "The Spirit of Place in the Western World," in James A. Swann (ed.) **The Power of Place** (Wheaton, Ill.: Quest Books, 1991), pp. 15-16.

[3] Eduardo Matos Moctezuma, "The Aztec Main Pyramid," in Richard Townsend (ed.) **The Ancient Americas: Art from Sacred Landscapes** (Chicago: Chicago Art Institute, 1992), p. 191.

[4] J. Donald Hughes, op. cit., p. 25.

[5] See, for example, Natasha Peterson, **Sacred Sites: A Traveler's Guide to North America's Most Powerful Mystical Landscapes** (Chicago: Contemporary Books, 1988).

[6] The text of the speech is contained in Diane Ravitch (ed.) **The American Reader** (New York: Harper Perennial, 1991), p. 333.

[7] Kathleen Norris, **Dakota: A Spiritual Geography** (New York: Ticknor and Fields, 1993), pp. 1-2.

[8] **New York Times Book Review**, February 14, 1993, p. 8; February 28, 1993, p. 7; February 14, 1993, p. 18. See also Edward F. Bergman **The Spiritual Traveler: New York City** (Mahwah, N.J.: Hidden Spring, 2001).

[9] Robert Bellah, et. al. **Habits of the Heart** (New York: Harper & Row, 1986), p. 277.

The Cathedral of the Assumption, Louisville.

CATHEDRALS

Any cathedral throughout the world is the central church of a diocese, the seat of a bishop, a tangible link back to the earliest church, and to the energies and call of Jesus Christ. There are about 160 Catholic cathedrals in the United States alone. A cathedral is an emblem, a pointer to the call of the Gospel. It is a place of solemnity and life, celebration and service, and calls its people to faith, hope and charity. In the Middle Ages especially, cathedrals became centers not only for prayer, but also for hospitality, care of the poor, morality plays and civic festivals. Cathedral schools often became the core from which grew the great universities of Europe.

When they are at their best, cathedrals are comprehensive centers of the intensity of life. Within them and around them, worship is celebrated; arts flourish; critical community and world issues may be addressed; the creative word shapes human lives; a wide range of human needs and hungers are nurtured; toleration and understanding bloom; and presences of the past are invoked even as images of the future are envisioned.

These great cathedral edifices are testaments to the ongoing search of humanity for that which transcends — even while respecting — the immediate and the ordinary. They are also testimonies to the realities of divine grace and the endurance of the human spirit. As Catholicism came to the American frontier in the late eighteenth and early nineteenth centuries, the stabilizing force of the church and the deep symbolizations of the cathedrals took on special power and significance. The old cathedrals that punctuate the landscape of Kentucky and southern Indiana take a pride of place on the historical landscape of this region of the American heartland.

THE ANTEBELLUM CATHEDRALS
BARDSTOWN
LOUISVILLE
VINCENNES

COVINGTON
EVANSVILLE
INDIANAPOLIS
LEXINGTON
OWENSBORO

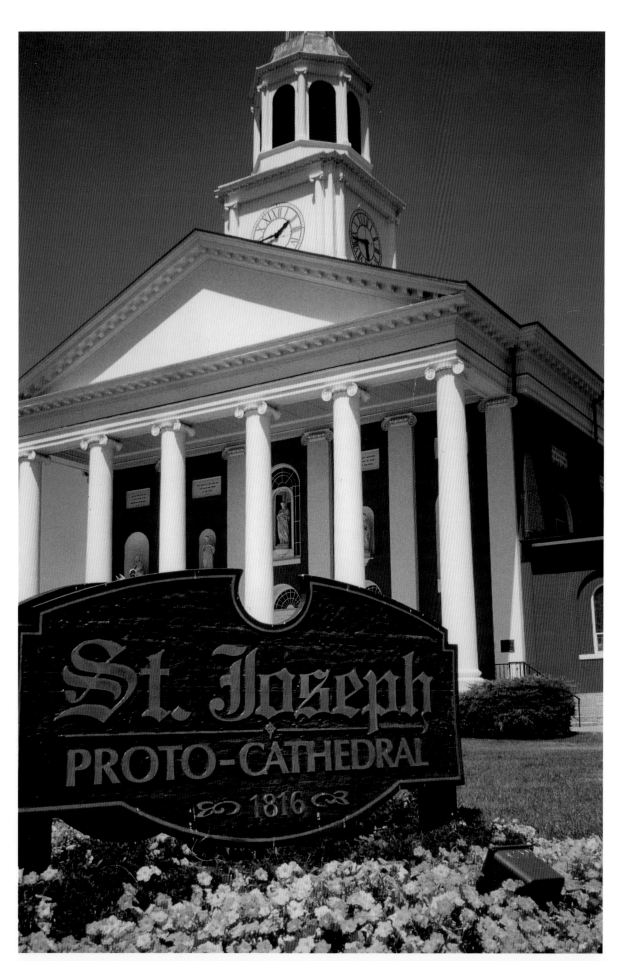

Benedict Joseph Flaget (1763-1850) was the saintly primal bishop of the American West. He arrived in Bardstown as bishop in 1811, remaining in that stately municipality until moving to Louisville thirty years later. A man of great wisdom, charm and holiness, Flaget lived a life of great simplicity and rugged pioneer labor. A diplomatic and ecumenical leader for his day, the French-born Flaget helped to cast the mode for a Catholicism that is loyal, reverent and creative.

Construction on Bishop Flaget's great "Cathedral in the Wilderness" — to a design of John Rogers — began in 1816. Most of the bricks were fired on site and the interior is adorned with many pictures and artifacts that were royal and papal gifts. The building's grand dedication took place on August 8, 1819. Today the church is designated as "Proto-Cathedral" which denotes its status as the first cathedral in the area. It is also called more popularly, "the old Cathedral." By action of the Holy See in August, 2001, the building was raised to the dignity of a minor basilica. There are two others in Kentucky: the Abbey Church at Gethsemani, and the Cathedral at Covington. Indiana has two basilicae: the University Church at Notre Dame and the Old Cathedral at Vincennes.

The right front portal of the Bardstown Basilica, showing fanlight window, column and Sacred Heart of Jesus statue.

St. Francis Xavier Basilica (known as The Old Cathedral) in Vincennes, Indiana, houses the earliest Christian congregation in the state. Begun in 1826 and completed by 1841, the church served the largely French congregation and also was cathedral church for the diocese of Vincennes (formed in 1834 – taken from the Bardstown diocese). It retained this cathedral status until the seat of the diocese was moved to Indianapolis in 1898.

Within the crypt of the Old Cathedral are buried the first four bishops of Vincennes, including its' first prelate, Simon Bruté (1779-1839), originally a physician; and its second Celestine de la Hailandière, (1798-1882), originally an attorney. The cathedral features a wine-glass pulpit as well as several statues such as the regal Madonna and Child.

Before the Old Cathedral at Vincennes stands a statue of Father Pierre Gibault (1735-1802) designed by Albin Polasek. An early pastor at Vincennes, Gibault had aided George Rogers Clark in winning the allegiance of many of the area's citizens to the American cause during the Revolution. This did not please Jean-Olivier Briand, his bishop in Quebec.

The center of Catholicism in America's oldest inland diocese, Louisville's Cathedral of the Assumption is a vibrant Catholic parish. It serves the needs of the inner-city, while also hosting inter-faith events. Ceremonial visits have been made here by the Dalai Lama, Muhammad Ali and Nobel Laureate Elie Wiesel. Here on February 26, 1862, Bishop Martin John Spalding conducted a memorial service for those who had perished — both Union and Confederate — in recent battles of the Civil War. And here on April 14, 1941, young Thomas Merton made the first of his many visits to the church. Here, members of the Louisville Orchestra perform during re-opening festivities of November 21, 1994. Extensive restoration work was accomplished through the ongoing work of an innovative Cathedral Heritage Foundation.

One of the nation's great urban cathedrals, the Cathedral of the Assumption in Louisville — designed by William Keely — has stood at its Fifth Street location since 1852. The parish traces its foundation to 1805, while Jefferson was the American president. Two previous buildings have served the congregation: one near Tenth and Main from 1811 to 1830; and a predecessor on this same site from 1830 to 1850.

In a view from the 1890's, the Cathedral is seen in the days when it served a largely residential neighborhood. Over a generation earlier, city historian Ben Casseday wrote in his 1852 **History of Louisville:** *The city south of Jefferson Street is very beautiful. The streets are lined on either side with large and elegant shade trees...An impression of elegant ease everywhere characterizes this part of the city.*

The final resting place of Bishop Benedict Joseph Flaget is in the Chapel of the Bishops in the crypt of Louisville's Cathedral of the Assumption.

GLEANINGS FROM THE HISTORY OF LOUISVILLE'S CATHEDRAL OF THE ASSUMPTION

▧ LATE SUMMER 1832 - SELFLESS SACRIFICE AND SERVICE

The cholera was ravaging Louisville. Four volunteer Sisters of Charity of Nazareth arrived in the city to provide nursing services: Sisters Margaret Bamber, Martha Drury, Martina Beaven and Hilaria Bamber. Along with Fr. Robert Abell, the pastor of the St. Louis Church (on the site of today's Cathedral), the sisters gathered with Bishop Flaget in the Fifth Street church. They knelt in silence; the Bishop made an act of consecration; they kissed the floor. Then all went out to stand by the bedsides of the stricken to assist in any way they were needed, physically or spiritually.

> Derived from account in Annals 1832
> Archives of the Sisters of Charity of Nazareth

▧ SUMMER 1860 - OPPOSING THE POLKA

In the Journal kept by Louisville Bishop Martin John Spalding we learn that on Trinity Sunday, June 3, 1860, he preached at the Cathedral on the Holy Trinity. Speaking of himself in the third person, Bishop Spalding then notes: *"He pronounced a severe invective and warning against the current fashionable dances — waltzes, polkas etc."*

> From Journal of Martin John Spalding
> University of Notre Dame Archives

▧ AUTUMN 1862 - A BISHOP GRUMPY OVER TABLE TALK

While Louisville experienced its most tumultuous time of the Civil War, the autumn of 1862, U.S. General William Rosecrans a convert to Catholicism came through the city. His brother Sylvester Rosecrans was auxiliary bishop of Cincinnati, and Bishop Spalding invited both of them to the Cathedral rectory for dinner on October 30. Bishop Spalding confided to his Journal:

"The General ingrossed (sic) the whole conversation after having been politely toasted by me along with his brother, thrusting on us the odious subject of abolition and growing quite excited....his Brother sitting by in sullen silence. All believed it to be in exceeding bad taste to say the least...."

From Journal of
Martin John Spalding
November 1, 1862
University of Notre Dame Archives

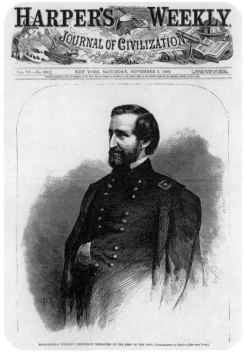

General William Rosecrans.

■ SURPRISING SACRAMENTAL RECORDS

The Bloody Monday Riots of August 6, 1855 were the result of a virulent campaign in Louisville by the Know-Nothing Party against immigrants in general and Catholics in particular. Over a score of citizens died of violence on that day. It may come as a surprise to know that, according to sacramental records at the Cathedral, two weddings were held in the church (with Fr. John Bekkers presiding) the very morning of Bloody Monday — this at a time that some were suspicious the Catholics were hiding men and munitions in the building.

Catherine Spalding, foundress of the Sisters of Charity of Nazareth. In the 1830's she was a member of St. Louis Church.

As one searches the baptismal records of this era, there are to be found at the Cathedral over 100 baptisms of enslaved persons. Usually the word "servant" is placed in the record; but on occasion the euphemism slips away and the word "slave" appears.

A striking entry from the baptismal records of the Cathedral of the Assumption of September 18, 1864 shows that Fr. David Russell baptized Edward David (slave of Henry Hagan).

The baptismal entry of July 29, 1936, shows that Fr. Herman J. Lammers administered the sacrament to Joseph Rainey Bethea, a convert to Catholicism. The ceremony took place at the Jefferson County Jail. Two weeks later, Bethea was taken to Owensboro and executed by hanging, the last public execution in America. The date was August 14, 1936.

Bishop Martin John Spalding. He lived at the rectory next to the Cathedral.

◆◆
◆◆
One of the most remarkable structures in all of Kentucky is
Covington's Cathedral Basilica of
the Assumption. The building is
French Gothic in style, and drew
much of its inspiration from St.
Denis and Notre Dame at Paris.
Leon Couquard was the main architect, but the west facade is largely
the work of David Davis. The
church was begun in 1894, opened
for services in 1901, and its main
facade finished in 1910.

The Covington Cathedral houses one of the largest stained-glass windows in existence. It also is home to major paintings by noted artist Frank Duveneck.

Covering much of southwestern Indiana, the Diocese of Evansville was formed by Pope Pius XII in 1944. St. Benedict Parish in Evansville was established in 1912. Its church building opened in 1927, and in April, 1999 it was designated the Evansville Cathedral.

Altar and Baldachin at St. Benedict's.

Though the many impressive churches of Indianapolis are not part of the geographical range of this book, its Cathedral of Sts. Peter and Paul is included here. It is the mother-church or cathedral for scores of Catholic structures in southern Indiana. The line of the Archdiocese of Indianapolis extends south to the Ohio River, and includes southern Indiana counties in the Louisville metro area. The building was completed in 1907. Neo-Classic in style, it was designed by William Renwick.

The newest and most strikingly modern of Kentucky's Catholic cathedrals is that of Christ the King in Lexington, opened in 1957 to a design of George Schulte. Lexington — and much of southeastern Kentucky — was constituted a diocese by Pope John Paul II in 1988. One of the interior distinctions of the church are Stations of the Cross painted by Carl John Zimmerman.

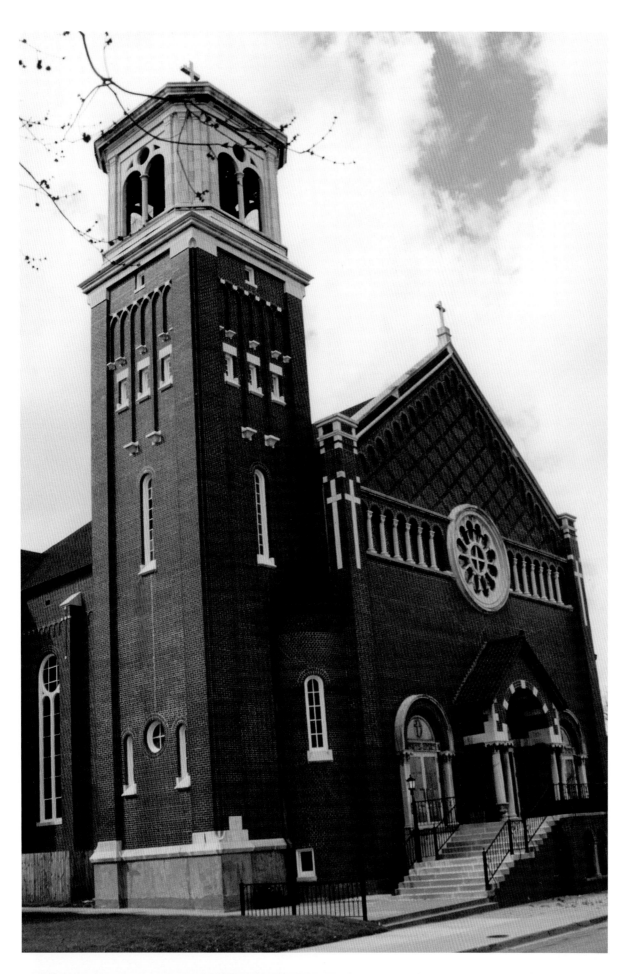

By action of Pope Pius XI in late 1937, western Kentucky was constituted a diocese with Owensboro as the see city. St. Stephen Parish, which had begun as a mission congregation in 1822 (with parish status given in 1839), was named the site of the cathedral. The current structure was opened for worship in 1924.

St. Rose Church and Cemetery near Springfield, Kentucky.

Parish Churches

Across the United States of America, Catholic faith, worship and life are vitally and vibrantly expressed in the parish, that family of families of Christian faith. In all, the United States numbers about 20,000 Catholic parishes. In Kentucky there are 300 such units (297 to be exact with the figures from the 2000 Official Catholic Directory). In southern Indiana (for the purposes of this text mostly those areas south of the city of Indianapolis) there are approximately 100 additional parishes.

This chapter showcases a few selected parish churches from those approximately 400 in the geographical area that is our focus in these pages. For the most part — and with only a few exceptions — the buildings shown here are of a more historic variety, that is, they were constructed before the First World War. In some smaller towns, these structures are still the single architectural expression of Catholic identity. In other towns (and certainly in the larger cities), these older parish churches have assumed or are assuming landmark status.

These churches are now becoming rarities on the urban landscape as more modern suburban styles have proliferated since the Second World War. Just as is the case with the pre-war churches, some of these are excellent; some are not. As we enter the twenty-first century many of these older churches represent — especially for younger generations who have not known such formal or ornate styles — awesome places. Many of these structures are old-worldly and almost other-worldly. They can offer a sense of special reverence, of history, and even at times, of grandeur.

PARISH CHURCHES
LOUISVILLE CITY CENTER

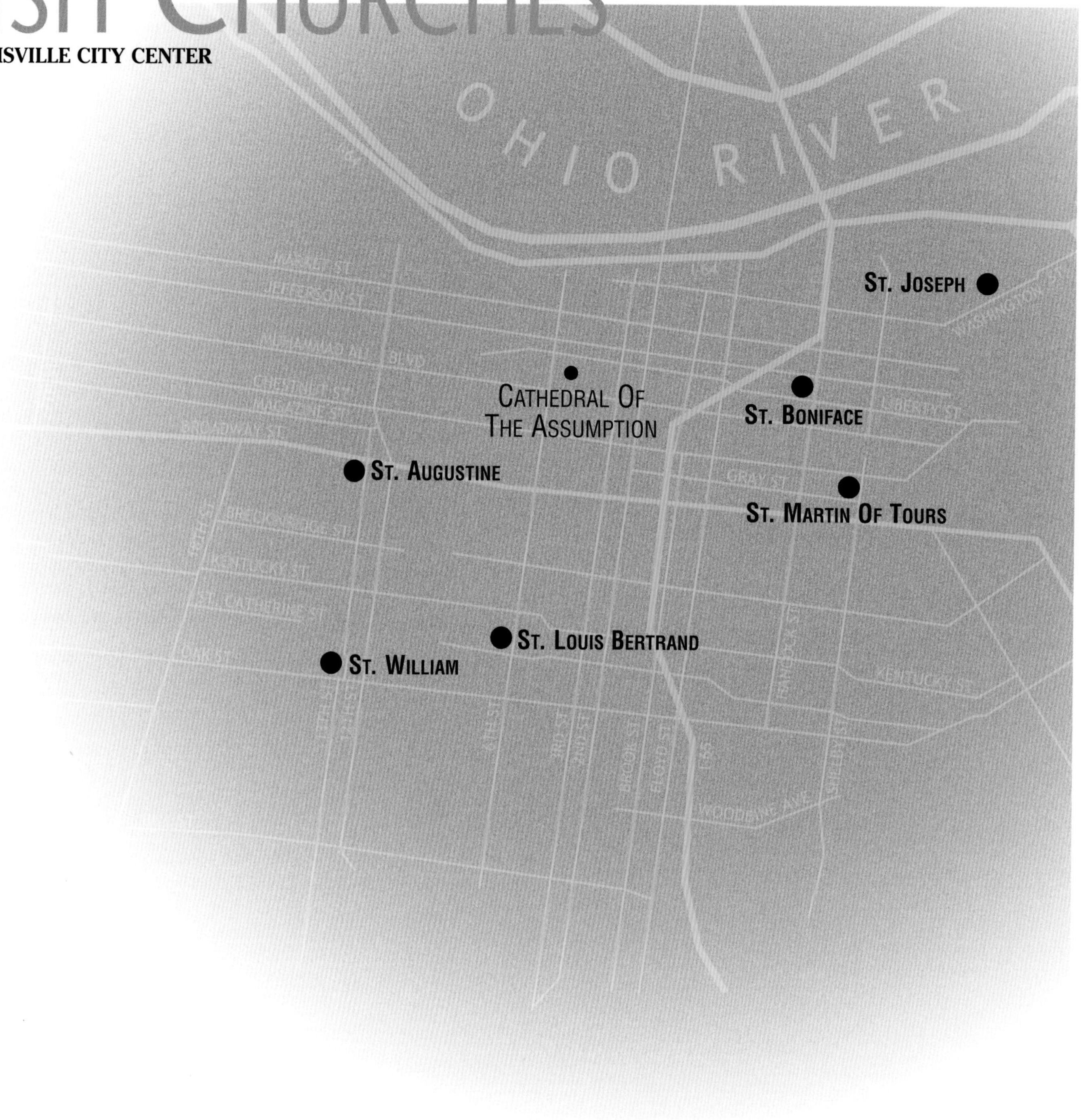

OHIO RIVER

ST. JOSEPH ●

● CATHEDRAL OF THE ASSUMPTION

ST. BONIFACE ●

● ST. AUGUSTINE

● ST. MARTIN OF TOURS

● ST. LOUIS BERTRAND

● ST. WILLIAM

ST. AUGUSTINE
ST. BONIFACE
ST. JOSEPH
ST. LOUIS BERTRAND
ST. MARTIN OF TOURS
ST. WILLIAM

St. Augustine is the mother-church of African-American parishes in Louisville. It was established by Fr. John Lancaster Spalding, one of the founders of Catholic University of America in Washington. Though the parish dates to 1865, the current church on Broadway near Thirteenth was dedicated September 10, 1911. A financial sponsor of the church — a visitor in the summer of 1905 — was Saint Katharine Drexel.

St. William Parish was founded by Bishop William G. McCloskey in 1901 and placed the cornerstone for this building the next year at 13th and Oak Streets.

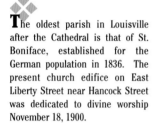

The oldest parish in Louisville after the Cathedral is that of St. Boniface, established for the German population in 1836. The present church edifice on East Liberty Street near Hancock Street was dedicated to divine worship November 18, 1900.

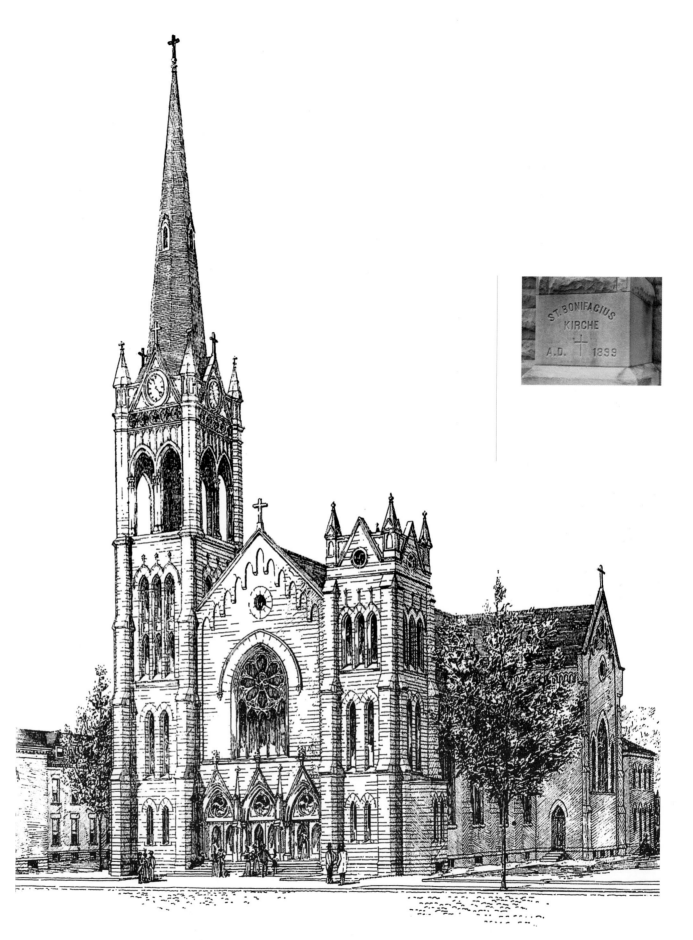

Yet another German congregation — this one founded in 1866 and long under the care of Franciscan Fathers — is that of St. Joseph on East Washington Street in the Butchertown neighborhood of Louisville. The church was dedicated September 12, 1886 and is widely known both for its twin spires and for its intricate wood carving at the altars. The spires rise 185 feet above the ground.

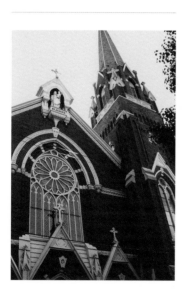

The interior of St. Joseph Church as it appeared about the time of the turn of the last century.

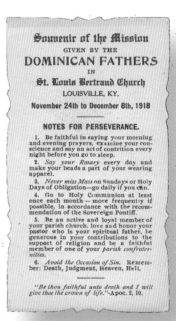

St. Louis Bertrand Parish was established in 1866, largely to serve an Irish population. It has been from the beginning in the care of the Dominican Fathers. Some dapper Dominicans are seen here from about the time of the First World War. The present structure was dedicated December 22, 1872 and stands at Sixth and St. Catherine Streets. The latter street, incidentally is believed to have been named in honor of the founder of the Sisters of Charity, Catherine Spalding.

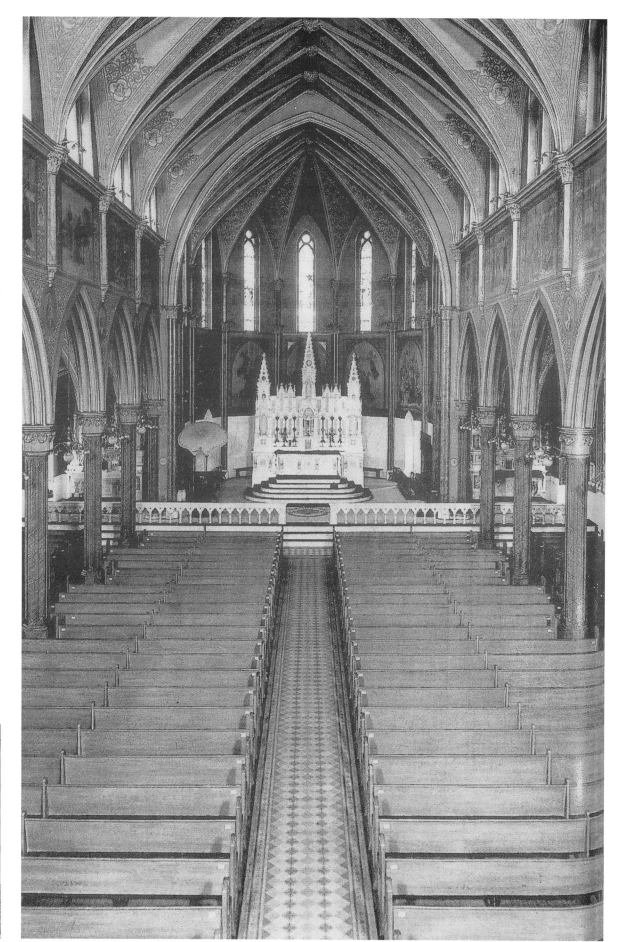

The Church of St. Louis Bertand as it appeared about the time of the First World War.

The congregation of St. Martin of Tours was established in 1853 for the growing German population of Louisville. Its' parish church, at Shelby and Gray Streets, opened the following year on August 20. Though subsequently enlarged, the structure remains in many ways as it was at the time of its opening. The building came under threat of mob violence during the anti-immigrant riot of 1855.

One of the remarkable features of St. Martin Church are the skeletal relics of two early Christian martyrs. The relics of St. Bonosa (shown here) and St. Magnus rest in glass beneath side altars. These rare relics arrived in Louisville on New Year's Eve, 1901.

Even today, the building that was once the parish school gives evidence of the use of the German language in the parish.

PARISH CHURCHES
LOUISVILLE CITY-WIDE

ST. ALOYSIUS

MOTHER OF GOOD COUNSEL

OUR LADY
ST. CECILIA
ST. ANTHONY

CATHEDRAL OF THE ASSUMPTION

ST. LEONARD

HOLY SPIRIT

ST. MARTIN DE PORRES

ST. BRIGID
ST. THERESE
ST. ELIZABETH

ST. FRANCES OF ROME
ST. JAMES
ST. AGNES

HOLY NAME

ST. RITA

HOLY NAME
HOLY SPIRIT
MOTHER OF GOOD COUNSEL
OUR LADY
ST. AGNES
ST. ALOYSIUS
ST. ANTHONY
ST. BRIGID
ST. CECILIA
ST. ELIZABETH
ST. FRANCES OF ROME
ST. JAMES
ST. LEONARD
ST. MARTIN DE PORRES
ST. RITA
ST. THERESE

The Church of the Holy Spirit on Louisville's Lexington Road opened February 22, 1955. Its architecture reflects the style of several models: old St. Joseph Cathedral in Bardstown, Bruton Parish Church in Williamsburg, Virginia and the Naval Academy Chapel in Annapolis, Maryland. The adjoining rectory reflects the lines of the Old Kentucky Home in Bardstown. The parish itself dates to 1937.

❖ **F**ounded in Louisville's South End in 1891, Holy Name Parish constructed this Romanesque style structure in 1912 to a design of J. J. Gaffney. The dedication took place October 27 of that year. Archival photos show the church about 1940 as it prepared for its golden anniversary.

The congregation of Our Lady was organized in 1839 by Stephen Badin, first priest ordained in the United States. The parish began as a center for French immigrants and was initially called Notre Dame du Port. The church on Rudd Avenue in Louisville's Portland neighborhood was opened in 1879 using the same bricks from the initial 1841 building. An interior perspective shows the church as it appeared about 1939.

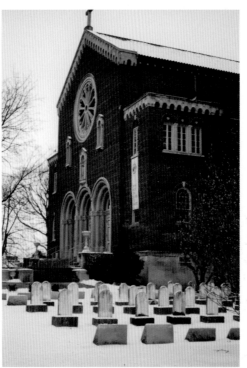

The congregation of St. Agnes in Louisville's Highlands traces its earliest roots to 1873. Parish status was granted in 1885, and since 1892 the parish has been in the care of the Passionist Fathers. Construction of the present church on Newburg Road began in 1927 with dedication taking place February 19, 1928. A noted internal feature of the building is a bas-relief frieze of over 100 children with an inscription beginning Laudate pueri Dominum: Children, praise the Lord.

The date is uncertain, but the story is a beguiling one. The third parish church of St. Aloysius in Pewee Valley was dedicated in 1914. As **The Record** told the tale on May 10, 1923, at some point after the church opened, it acquired a highly-placed admirer. Auto magnate Henry Ford was coming through on the mainline of the L&N railroad between Louisville and Cincinnati. The tracks pass directly in front of St. Aloysius. Mr. Ford was struck by the beauty of the church and its locale. He called it "the little Irish church" and declared that no other church he had seen in his American travels so nearly resembled the stone churches of Ireland. He ordered photographs made and sent a set to the pastor. "They will always be kept as a treasure," **The Record** predicted. Alas, a search of parish and diocesan files failed to produce these original photographic gems. A new church now serves the parish, but this one still proudly stands.

❖ **S**t. Anthony Church on Market Street and 23rd in Louisville was established for a German population in 1867 and its present church dedicated in 1887.

Another church in Louisville built in the basilica style was that of St. Brigid in the Highlands. The church was dedicated October 5, 1913.

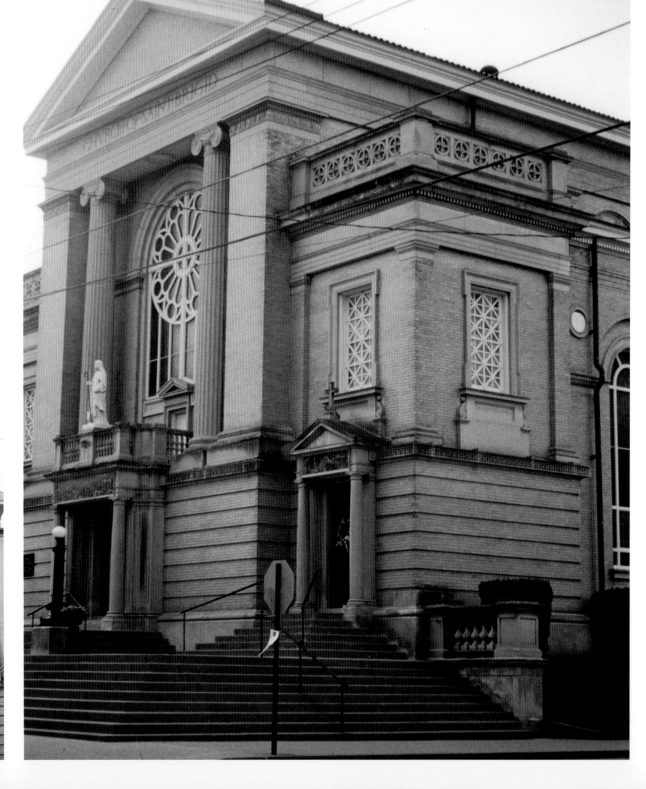

St. Cecilia Church in Louisville's Portland neighborhood was dedicated in 1910.

St. Elizabeth of Hungary Church on Burnett Avenue was dedicated September 2, 1906.

A jewel-box of a parish church is that of St. Frances of Rome, founded in 1887. The church on Payne Street was dedicated on October 2, 1887. This photo is probably from the 1940's.

◆ **St.** James Parish on Bardstown Road and Edenside in Louisville's Highlands was established in 1906. The church, in Spanish Revival style, was dedicated on December 21, 1913.

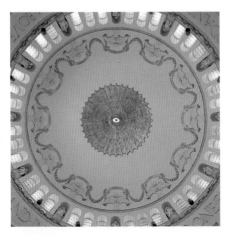

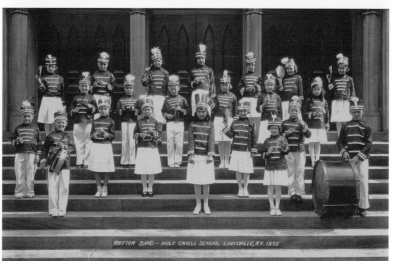

The parish of St. Martin de Porres was originally called Holy Cross when it was founded in 1895. Its Tudor Gothic church was blessed for use March 10, 1929 at 32nd and Broadway.

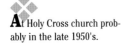
At Holy Cross church probably in the late 1950's.

The interior of old Holy Cross Church as it appeared in the 1920's.

Built in Spanish Mission Revival style, the Church of St. Therese stands on Louisville's Schiller Avenue. It was dedicated June 30, 1929.

St. Rita Church on Louisville's Preston Highway used this wooden frame structure from its dedication on February 26, 1922 until the 1950's.

Mother Of Good Counsel, one of the churches built just before the Second Vatican Council.

St. Leonard Church, built in 1960, was in many ways typical of post-war suburban parish growth.

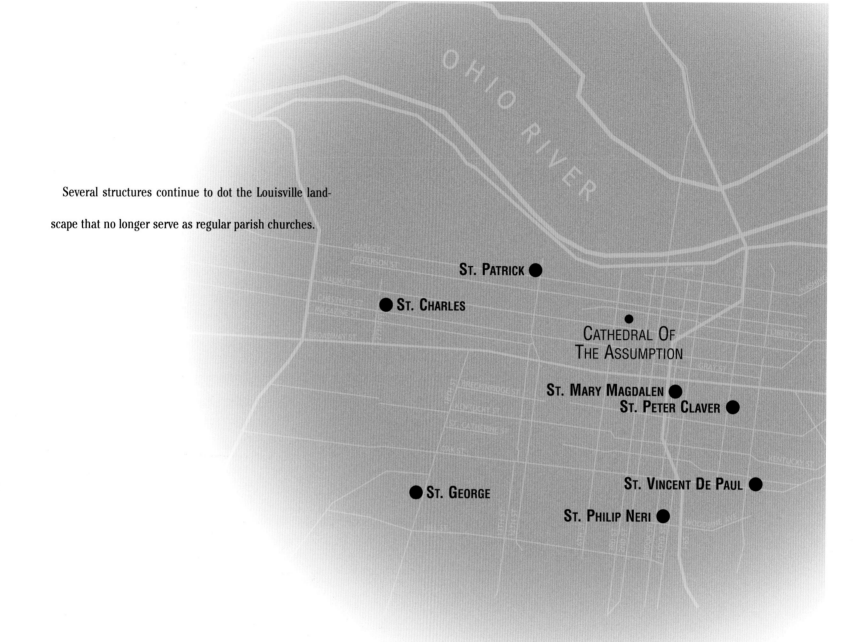

Several structures continue to dot the Louisville landscape that no longer serve as regular parish churches.

ST. PATRICK ●

● ST. CHARLES

●
CATHEDRAL OF
THE ASSUMPTION

ST. MARY MAGDALEN ●
ST. PETER CLAVER ●

ST. VINCENT DE PAUL ●

● ST. GEORGE

ST. PHILIP NERI ●

ST. CHARLES
ST. GEORGE
ST. MARY MAGDALEN
ST. PATRICK
ST. PETER CLAVER
ST. PHILIP NERI
ST. VINCENT DE PAUL

St. Charles Church, in the basilica style, was opened May 19, 1912, at 27th and Chestnut streets.

The Church of St. George – no longer in Catholic parochial service – was turned 90° on its axis. It is shown here in a 1937 view.

Detail – St. Philomena.

◆ In the church of St. Mary Magdalen on Louisville's Brook Street, a small plaque on a back pew reads:

> John F. Kennedy
> 1917-1963
> First Catholic President
> 1961-1963
> Attended Mass Here
> October 14, 1962

Historians will take note that as of this day, the Cuban Missile Crisis was about to begin.

◆ A devotional alcove at St. Mary Magdalen church highlights Our Lady of Perpetual Help (above) and a recumbant statue of St. Philomena (below).

St. Patrick Church at 13th and Market streets was dedicated in 1863.

St. Peter Claver Parish, closed in 2001, was an African-American congregation that met in this church on Lampton Street. The founding of the church was made possible in part through the generosity of Mother (now Saint) Katharine Drexel. It was dedicated February 24, 1907.

The pastor of St. Philip Neri parish from its founding in 1897 was Fr. Oscar Pacific Ackerman, who remained at his post until his death in 1925. The Church of St. Philip Neri was opened in 1899, largely through the generosity of the pastor's father, Philip Ackerman. The latter was a partner in the Senn and Ackerman Brewing Company which in 1900 was the second largest brewing enterprise in Louisville.

Founded in 1878, Louisville's St. Vincent de Paul parish on Shelby Street, built this modified Tudor Gothic church and it was dedicated October 7, 1888.

PARISH CHURCHES

THE KENTUCKY HOLY LAND

The Kentucky Holy Land is a designation now widely used to designate the three historic counties of Marion, Nelson and Washington in central Kentucky, about an hour's drive from Louisville. Pope Pius VII established America's first inland diocese at Bardstown in 1808, with Benedict Joseph Flaget, an exile from the French Revolution, as the first bishop of the West. On the same day, the pope also constituted dioceses in the cities of Boston, New York and Philadelphia.

The vast territory of the primal diocese covered land that would eventually become several states. It would be carved over the intervening centuries into well over thirty additional dioceses, including Cincinnati, Chicago, Nashville and Indianapolis.

The Holy Land had been settled — beginning largely in the 1780's — by lay Maryland Catholics of British stock. As has been noted, their first parishes were lay-founded; their first seminary began its life on a flatboat on the Ohio River; one of their first colleges began life in an old distillery building. These were truly a resourceful and vibrant people. The clerical leaders of these stalwart pioneers were at the outset predominantly French.

An amazing array of institutions sprang from this Kentucky soil in the early nineteenth century: a seminary (St. Thomas); a monastery (Gethsemani); three native sisterhoods (The Sisters of Loretto, The Sisters of Charity of Nazareth and the Dominican Sisters); colleges, academies, and perhaps the most famous landmark of all, St. Joseph Cathedral in Bardstown.

The seat of the Bardstown diocese was shifted in 1841 to the rapidly growing city of Louisville. But this did not occur before Bardstown had served as a cradle to Catholicism in much of the Midwest and upper South, and had exported Catholic leadership across the United States.

FAIRFIELD
HOLY CROSS
LEBANON
NEW HAVEN
NEW HOPE
ST. CHARLES
ST. ROSE
ST. THOMAS FARM

Kentucky Catholicism's primal parish, that of Holy Cross, was founded in 1785. An earlier structure was opened in 1792, and the current building (built in part by hand, legend says, by pioneer priest Charles Nerinckx) opened for divine service in 1823. Today the church and its surrounding cemetery are proud landmarks of Marion County.

Lebanon in Marion County has been home to St. Augustine Parish since its establishment in 1815. From this congregation came two famous bishop-theologians of the 19th century: Martin John Spalding and John Lancaster Spalding. The current church opened in 1871 and is shown in this rare interior image of 1908.

A rare interior photograph from the Golden Jubilee of Father Peter De Fraine at St. Augustine Church, Lebanon, Kentucky, in 1901.

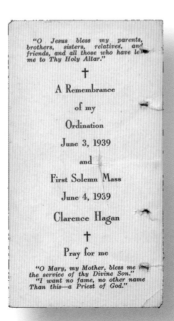

"O Jesus bless my parents, brothers, sisters, relatives, and friends, and all those who have led me to Thy Holy Altar."

✝

A Remembrance
of my
Ordination
June 3, 1939
and
First Solemn Mass
June 4, 1939

Clarence Hagan

✝

Pray for me

"O Mary, my Mother, bless me in the service of thy Divine Son."
"I want no fame, no other name Than this—a Priest of God."

◈ **T**he funeral at St. Catherine Church at New Haven of Fr. Clarence Hagan, military chaplain from the Archdiocese of Louisville. He was killed in Italy in 1945 in an attempt to minister to a wounded soldier.

In Marion County, the parish of St. Charles dates its beginnings to 1786. Its current church building opened on August 15, 1905.

One of Kentucky's most historic churches is that of St. Rose in Washington County, near Springfield. Since its founding in 1806, it has been the work of the Dominican Fathers, and was, in fact, the first Dominican foundation in the United States. While portions of the building date to 1808, the main edifice was built in 1855, being dedicated August 4 of that year. The octagonal bell tower stands as a highly distinctive feature in rural Kentucky.

The parish of St. Michael at Fairfield, established in 1792, has a distinctive baptismal font.

❖ The oldest standing Catholic church building in Kentucky is that of the parish of St. Thomas (often called St. Thomas Farm) near Bardstown. Established in 1812, the parish built the current church in 1816. The building itself is in many ways a replica of the Paca Street Church in Baltimore, homeland for the early Kentucky Catholic settlers.

❖ On these historic grounds there lived Bishops Benedict Joseph Flaget and John Baptist David. Here also the first St. Thomas Seminary (see p. 230) began its life in the old log house still standing. And here, late in 1812, the Sisters of Charity of Nazareth made their first foundation.

The Church of St. Vincent de Paul in New Hope (Nelson County) was dedicated in April, 1890, and is noted for its wood-carved altar.

PARISH CHURCHES

KENTUCKY

CINCINNATI •

● **SACRED HEART** BELLEVUE

MUTTERGOTTES ●
COVINGTON

● **ST. PATRICK**
MAYSVILLE

GOOD SHEPHERD
FRANKFORT

LOUISVILLE ●

● **ANNUNCIATION** PARIS

● **ST. FRANCIS DE SALES**
WHITE SULPHUR

ST. PAUL ●
LEXINGTON

ST. THERESA ●
RHODELIA

ST. JOHN ● **ST. CLARE**
RINEYVILLE COLESBURG

ST. AGNES UNIONTOWN
● **ST. ANN**
MORGANFIELD

● **ST. SYLVESTER**
EAST BERNSTADT

● **ST. FRANCIS DE SALES**
PADUCAH

ST. JOSEPH ●
BOWLING GREEN

● **ST. JEROME**
FANCY FARM

● **ST. ANTHONY**
PINEVILLE

BELLEVUE
BOWLING GREEN
COLESBURG
COVINGTON
EAST BERNSTADT
FANCY FARM
FRANKFORT
LEXINGTON
MAYSVILLE
MORGANFIELD

PADUCAH
PARIS
PINEVILLE
RHODELIA
RINEYVILLE
UNIONTOWN
WHITE SULPHUR

An historically German parish in northern Kentucky is Sacred Heart (originally Herz Jesu) in Bellevue, near Covington. Special interior features of the 1892 structure are the colorful bas-relief altars and a striking depiction of the souls in purgatory.

One of the most historic churches in southern Kentucky is that of St. Joseph in Bowling Green. Built in 1862 the parish church continues strong today with liturgies in both English and Spanish.

This rare undated interior photo of St. Joseph Church comes from probably the very early 20th century. Special features to note include the Gothic wine-glass pulpit and highly articulated heavenly images of angels and saints.

Muttergottes — Mother of God — Church in downtown Covington represents yet another church built primarily for and by German immigrants to America. The church opened in 1871 to a design of the firm of Walter and Stewart. The Covington area is particularly rich in stately old parish structures.

Good Shepherd Church.

On the far right of the photo rises the steeple of Good Shepherd Church, the only Catholic house of worship in the Commonwealth's capital city of Frankfort. The parish was established in 1849 and built its' church in 1850. It sits across from the Public Library.

St. Paul Church in downtown Lexington was opened in 1865, the very year that saw the end of the American Civil War.

The imposing St. Patrick Church at Maysville, Kentucky was dedicated June 26, 1910. The pastor at the time envisioned it as destined to become a little replica of Notre Dame of Paris.

In far western Kentucky, in the heart of town, sits the well-known Church of St. Jerome at Fancy Farm. Here the annual summer picnic brings political leaders from across Kentucky for old-fashioned stump speeches. The church was dedicated November 29, 1893.

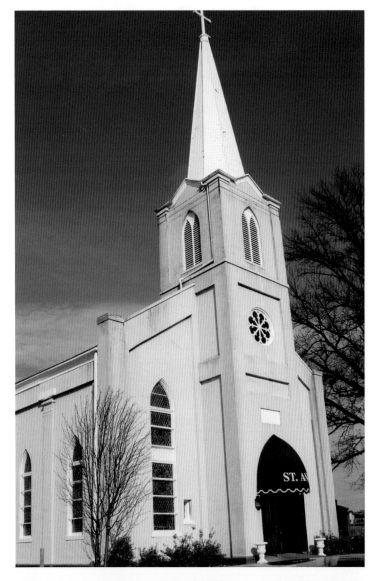

Early in the 19th century, many Catholics from the Kentucky Holy Land migrated to western Kentucky. St. Ann Church in Morganfield in Union County represents the vibrancy of faith in that area. The church was dedicated in March, 1878.

In the Kentucky Purchase area, in the city of Paducah, stands the stately Church of St. Francis de Sales. Construction on the twin-towered landmark began in 1899.

Annunciation Church in Paris, Bourbon County. This Bluegrass parish structure was dedicated in 1861.

The relatively low number of Catholics in eastern Kentucky often leads to church structures that are small, but elegant in their simplicity. Here are to be seen St. Anthony Church in Pineville in Bell County and the Church of St. Sylvester in East Bernstadt in Laurel County. Both are within the Lexington Diocese.

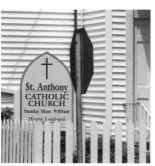

St. Agnes Church in Uniontown, near Morganfield, offers another example of the strength of Catholicism in this section of western Kentucky.

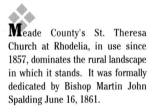

Meade County's St. Theresa Church at Rhodelia, in use since 1857, dominates the rural landscape in which it stands. It was formally dedicated by Bishop Martin John Spalding June 16, 1861.

One of Kentucky's primal Catholic congregations, St. Francis de Sales in White Sulphur (Scott County) traces its origins to 1786. As described in the church's history "That Troublesome Parish" by Ann Bolton Bevins and Reverend James R. O'Rourke, the parish knew stormy times, especially in its early years. The current church structure dates from 1820.

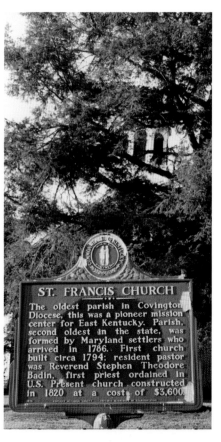

Catholicism at Rineyville in Hardin County has roots going back to the labors of pioneer priest Charles Nerinckx in 1812. St. John Church attained parish status in 1829 and opened its current structure for worship in 1898.

ST. CLARE CHURCH
BUILT 1874

The oldest Catholic congregation in Hardin County is that of St. Clare in Colesburg. The present church, built in 1874, sits in an idyllic setting. The parish cemetery is about a mile distant from the structure.

PARISH CHURCHES

SOUTHERN INDIANA

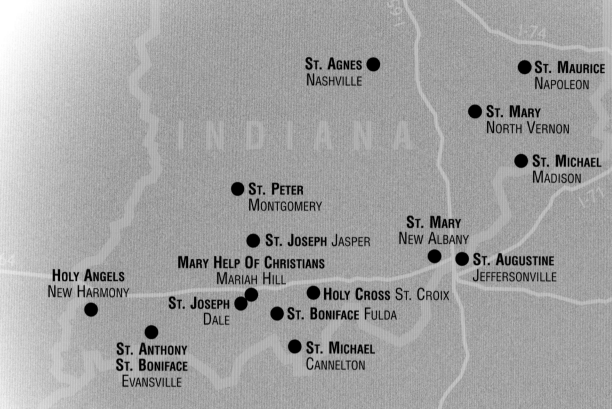

ST. AGNES
NASHVILLE

ST. MAURICE
NAPOLEON

ST. MARY
NORTH VERNON

ST. MICHAEL
MADISON

ST. PETER
MONTGOMERY

ST. JOSEPH JASPER

ST. MARY
NEW ALBANY

MARY HELP OF CHRISTIANS
MARIAH HILL

ST. AUGUSTINE
JEFFERSONVILLE

HOLY ANGELS
NEW HARMONY

ST. JOSEPH
DALE

HOLY CROSS ST. CROIX

ST. BONIFACE FULDA

ST. ANTHONY
ST. BONIFACE
EVANSVILLE

ST. MICHAEL
CANNELTON

CANNELTON
DALE
EVANSVILLE
FULDA
JASPER
JEFFERSONVILLE
MADISON
MARIAH HILL
MONTGOMERY

NAPOLEON
NASHVILLE
NEW ALBANY
NEW HARMONY
NORTH VERNON
ST. CROIX

St. Michael Church, dating from 1859, stands facing the Ohio River in Cannelton, in Perry County.

St. Joseph Church in Dale (Spencer County) was completed in 1909. Here it is seen in a late-winter sunset.

The German influence seems endless in the southern reaches of Indiana. The congregation of St. Boniface at Fulda (Spencer County) began in 1847 and constructed its own Gothic Revival structure for worship in 1866. The interior has a quiet solemnity.

An impressive structure by almost any standard, St. Joseph Church forms an extraordinary architectural exclamation point in the city of Jasper. The German parish was established in 1837, and the massive Romanesque Revival church, seating over a thousand, was completed in 1880.

Just across the Ohio River from downtown Louisville lies the city of Jeffersonville, Indiana, part of the Archdiocese of Indianapolis. St. Augustine parish was begun in Jeffersonville in 1851. Its present edifice, in Mission style, was built in 1905.

One of the oldest parishes in Indiana, St. Peter at Montgomery in Daviess County, was first gathered in 1818. In this locale, Fr. Edwin Sorin and the Brothers of the Holy Cross lived before heading north to begin the University of Notre Dame in 1842. The church structure is of red brick in Gothic Revival style. Its interior is enlived by some excellent glass and statuary (a Madonna and Child are shown here). At the building's summit stands a (modest) golden dome!

The town of Mariah Hill derives its name from Maria Hilpf, Mary Help (of Christians). This Romanesque Revival structure, was completed in 1865 for a congregation that had been founded about 1857.

In Madison, the old parish of St. Michael, founded in 1837, merged in 1993 with St. Mary Parish to create the Prince of Peace congregation. The original Gothic Revival church of St. Michael gratefully remains. It was designed by Madison resident Francis Costigan and finished in 1839. Alongside the church stands the rectory from about 1860. According to historian Joseph White, the original church may be the oldest example of Gothic Revival style of worship in Indiana.

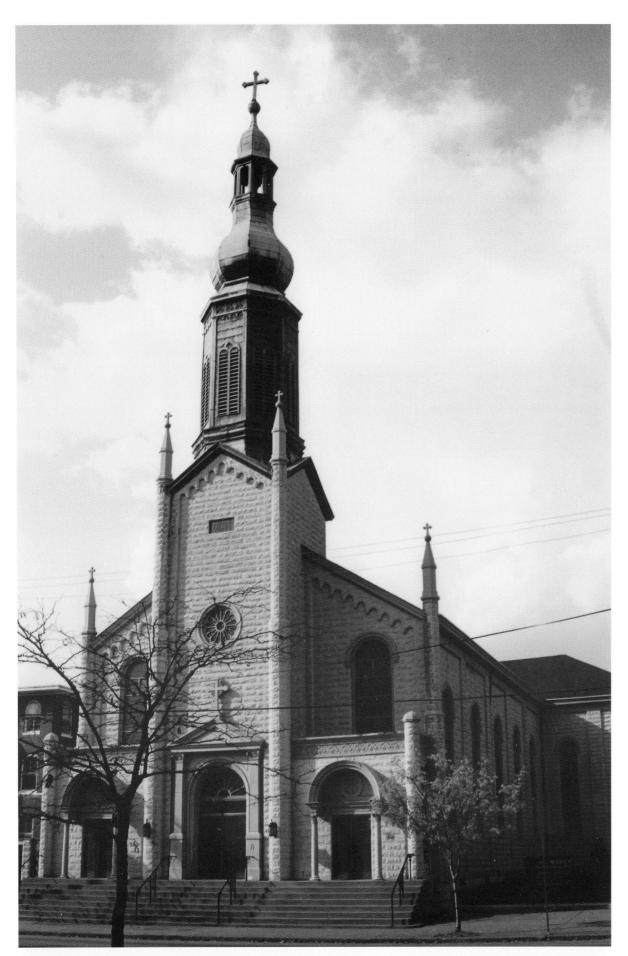

A remarkable number of churches in southern Indiana bear the title St. Mary... over a dozen in all. The Church of St. Mary in New Albany, across the Ohio River from Louisville's West End, was established in 1855. Its Romanesque Revival church with its distinctive onion-shaped spire was constructed in 1858.

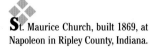 **St.** Maurice Church, built 1869, at Napoleon in Ripley County, Indiana.

Rustic in appearance, the Church of St. Agnes represents the Catholic tradition in the tourist center of Nashville in Brown County. It was built in 1940 and now features in addition to its sanctuary, an impressive outdoor shrine and worship area.

◆ **H**oly Angels Church in historic New Harmony is wood frame Gothic and was constructed in 1899.

◆ **T**he town of St. Croix in Perry County is home to the Romanesque Revival Holy Cross Church, erected in 1881 for a congregation formed in 1860.

One of the many St. Mary parishes in southern Indiana, and one of many Neo-Gothic churches in the area is to be found at North Vernon in Jennings County. Church construction began in 1861.

The interior of St. Mary Church at North Vernon.

St. Anthony of Padua Parish in Evansville was established in 1888.

St. Boniface Church in Evansville was built in 1881.

The Abbey Church at Gethsemani.

MONASTERIES AND MOTHERHOUSES

Since its early centuries, Christianity has revered the lives of its members who consecrate themselves in community to prayer, compassion and service, all patterned on the Christian Gospel. The very places where these dedicated persons have taken up their vowed lives have often come to be sought out as places of special spiritual intensity and peace. Here people of many different vocations and ways of life — and even variant religious traditions — have been welcomed with surpassing hospitality.

Kentucky and Indiana are singularly blessed with an abundance of these large, historic religious centers: monasteries, motherhouses and provincialates (headquarters of large and far-flung religious communities) and convents. The word "Motherhouse" in the title of this section is used in a wide sense, and not all the communities shown would use that particular phrase. In these pages we can provide images of only a selection of the larger sites.

There are many vowed and valued communities of prayer and service not shown in this section. The Sisters of Mercy are a major presence in the Louisville area, but their Motherhouse is in Cincinnati — beyond the geographical reach of these pages. But even closer to home, the area is rich in so many communities (like parishes in the previous chapter) that we cannot

begin to show them all. So we render quiet honor to a wide array of groups such as the Carmelite Sisters in Louisville; the Passionist Sisters in the Covington and Owensboro dioceses; the Sisters of St. Joseph the Worker in the Covington diocese; the Order of St. Clare near Evansville; the Fathers of Mercy at South Union. There are literally scores of others.

It should be noted that many American cities may have one such holy place within easy driving distance. Louisville has over half-a-dozen within about a leisurely 75 minute driving circle. Here is yet another example of the spiritual geography of this region — *a benediction of place.*

MONKS

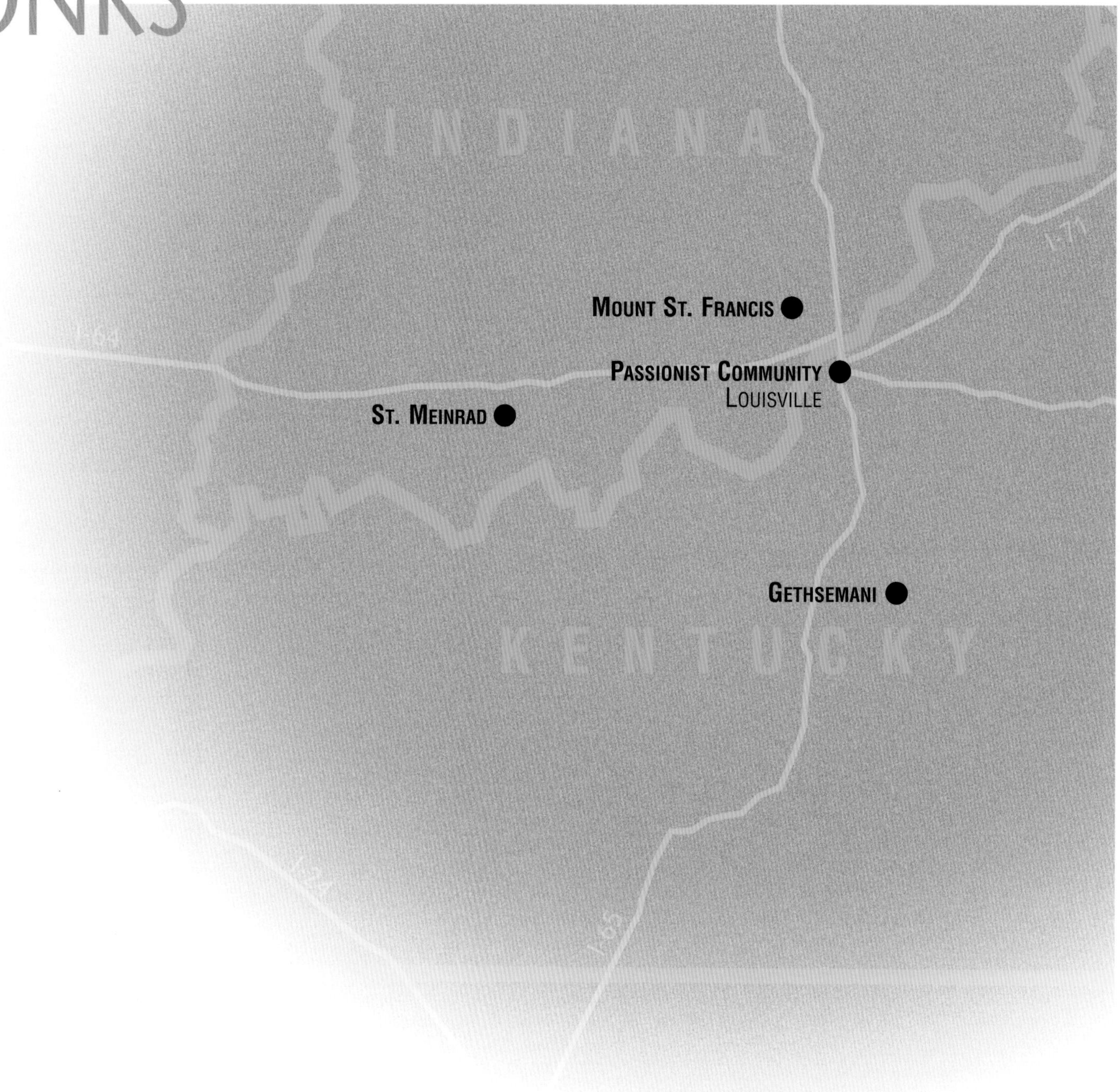

GETHSEMANI
LOUISVILLE
MOUNT SAINT FRANCIS
SAINT MEINRAD

The Archabbey Church at St. Meinrad opened in 1907. According to historian Joseph White, it was designed by a Franciscan Brother, Adrian Wewer who designed scores of Catholic churches across the United States in this era. The Romanesque Revival structure stands as one of the most impressive landmarks of southern Indiana.

A rare photo shows the main portal of the church during its construction.

Benedictine monks arrived in southern Indiana from the Abbey of Einsiedeln in Switzerland in 1854. They established a community that is today known as St. Meinrad Archabbey. A large and vibrant monastic community, St. Meinrad is home to a highly respected School of Theology as well as Abbey Press. The twin spires stand 168 feet high.

Dom Gregory de Wit, an exile from the Nazis, was responsible for the art work portraying St. Benedict and St. Meinrad, as well as the Christ in the central apse of the church.

The shrine of Monte Casino, a small chapel in sandstone in Romanesque style was constructed in 1870. Its construction is said to have been spurred by a promise made by monks at the time an epidemic was raging in the area.

The Franciscans (Order of Friars Minor Conventual) founded Mount St. Francis Friary near Floyds Knobs in Floyd County, Indiana in 1896. A Romanesque Revival church was built here in 1925 that features famous Franciscan saints and popes in its stained glass. A great benefactor in the early history at the Mount was internationally known actress Mary Anderson. The Mount today is a major retreat center and houses on its grounds the Mary Anderson Center.

❖ **T**he monastery of the Passionist Fathers on Louisville's Newburg Road was built in 1906. One legend relates that the columns may have come from an old plantation house in the area.

On December 18, 1848, an unusual site greeted anyone lingering about the Louisville Wharf. From the steamer Martha Washington there emerged over 40 monks from the Abbey of Meleray in France. These Trappist monks — part of the long Cistercian tradition — would go to the Louisville Cathedral to meet the venerable Bishop Flaget. Then they would make their way to Nelson County to found the Abbey of Gethsemani on land they had purchased from the Sisters of Loretto. Gethsemani remains today one of the oldest and largest American monasteries.

In the woods of Gethsemani is to be found the statue of Christ in Agony by Walker Hancock. The Christ is part of a set of figures designed as a memorial to Jonathan Daniels and others who gave their lives in the civil rights struggles in America in the 1950's and 60's.

THOMAS MERTON (1915-68)

Trappist monk, poet, social critic, and spiritual writer. Born in Prades, France. After education at Cambridge, and Columbia Univ., he entered Abbey of Gethsemani, Trappist, Ky., 1941; ordained as priest, 1949. His autobiography *The Seven Storey Mountain* (1948), earned international acclaim. He is buried in abbey cemetery.

Presented by Thomas Merton Center Foundation

A REVELATION

Merton had a sudden insight at this corner Mar. 18, 1958, that led him to redefine his monastic identity with greater involvement in social justice issues. He was "suddenly overwhelmed with the realization that I loved all these people...." He found them "walking around shining like the sun." *Conjectures of a Guilty Bystander*.

Presented by Thomas Merton Center Foundation

Merton's life – and burial site – are memorialized today in downtown Louisville on a state historical marker at Fourth Avenue and Muhammad Ali Boulevard.

In serene simplicity stands the traditional grave cross over the remains of Thomas Merton (1915-1968), the Abbey's most internationally renowned monk. The famous writer's monastic name was Louis, and thus he is remembered on the cross at his grave.

The Abbey Church was opened in 1866, immediately following the Civil War. A restoration of the 1960's revealed the original simplicity of the building's design.

SISTERS

KENTUCKY

CINCINNATI

SISTERS OF NOTRE DAME COVINGTON

SISTERS OF THE GOOD SHEPHERD FT. THOMAS

SISTERS OF DIVINE PROVIDENCE MELBOURNE

BENEDICTINE SISTERS OF ST. WALBURG MONASTERY VILLA HILLS

URSULINE SISTERS LOUISVILLE

SISTERS OF CHARITY OF NAZARETH
NAZARETH

DOMINICAN SISTERS SPRINGFIELD

URSULINE SISTERS MAPLE MOUNT

SISTERS OF LORETTO
NERINX

COVINGTON
FORT THOMAS
LOUISVILLE
MAPLE MOUNT
MELBOURNE
NAZARETH
NERINX
SPRINGFIELD
VILLA HILLS

The Church of the Seven Dolors at Loretto was built during the Civil War, opening for worship in 1864.

Founded in 1812, the Sisters of Loretto are among the oldest communities of sisters established in the United States. Their motherhouse grounds had long been the home of pioneer priests Stephen Badin and Charles Nerinckx. The latter, along with Ann Rhodes, first superior general, and her sister Mary, are revered as founders of the community.

A ceremony in the Motherhouse Church at Loretto in 1922.

Postulants — women aspiring to become sisters — arrive at the Loretto Mother-house in June, 1923.

◆ **S**ister of Loretto Henrietta Mudd along with Father John K. Viala pose for a formal photograph with children from "the colored school" at New Haven, Kentucky in 1885.

◆ **A**n unidentified Sister of Loretto with her class at St. Augustine School in Lebanon about 1897.

◆ **W**orkmen at Loretto bring in the melons for breakfast in 1922.

❖ **A** statue of Stephen Badin — containing a relic of his bone — stands on the Loretto grounds next to what is still called Badin's Cabin, built in 1816. Badin was the first priest ordained in the U.S., and is buried at the University of Notre Dame.

❖ **S**tatue of Reverend Charles Nerinckx.

❖ **S**acred Heart of Jesus statue at Loretto.

❖ **I**nside the Loretto cemetery. A detail from the Statues of the Seven Dolors of Mary.

TO THE
MEMORY OF
MOTHER
ANN RHODES
FIRST SUPERIOR GENERAL
DIED
DECEMBER 11, 1812
AGED 21 YEARS

Memorial to those who were once enslaved. Loretto Motherhouse Cemetery.

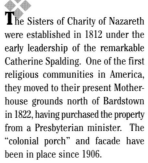
The Sisters of Charity of Nazareth were established in 1812 under the early leadership of the remarkable Catherine Spalding. One of the first religious communities in America, they moved to their present Motherhouse grounds north of Bardstown in 1822, having purchased the property from a Presbyterian minister. The "colonial porch" and facade have been in place since 1906.

A rare view of Nazareth and the main road leading to the Motherhouse and Church. The date is unknown, but is probably around 1890.

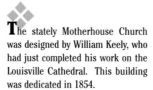

A Lourdes Grotto on the Mother-house grounds. The French inscrip-tion reads: I am the Immaculate Conception.

The stately Motherhouse Church was designed by William Keely, who had just completed his work on the Louisville Cathedral. This building was dedicated in 1854.

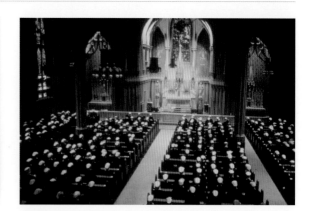

Ceremonies in the Motherhouse Church in 1956.

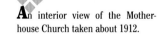
The Motherhouse Church sanctuary and altars in 1900.

An interior view of the Motherhouse Church taken about 1912.

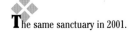
The same sanctuary in 2001.

The Sisters of Charity began their work of education as soon as they were founded. Throughout much of the 19th and 20th centuries, Nazareth Academy was a prestigious school that drew students from throughout the South. From the 1920's a Nazareth College stood on the grounds also, but it would eventually merge into what is now known as Spalding University in Louisville. Here are seen students of Nazareth Academy in 1892.

A visit to Nazareth by Archbishop Diomede Falconio, Apostolic Delegate to the United States, was the occasion for a grand welcome on September 13, 1911.

✦ **N**azareth Academy graduates of 1901.

✦ **N**azareth students serious about croquet. Date unknown.

✦ **N**azareth Academy students serious about tennis. Date unknown.

The Motherhouse of the Dominican Sisters near Springfield.

In 1822 the first American congregation of Dominican Sisters in the United States was founded in Washington County in Kentucky's Holy Land. The next year an academy was begun, eventually to be named for St. Catharine of Siena. In 1904 a terrible fire destroyed the motherhouse and academy, but the resourceful sisters rebuilt on Siena Heights. In 1931 St. Catharine Junior College was begun here, and in the same year an imposing new chapel was built.

As part of the reception of women into the Dominican community, they at one time dressed as brides before donning the religious habit. Such a ceremony is shown here in the St. Catharine Church, probably in the mid 1940's. A close-up of the circular window appears on p. 206.

A gathering of sisters at the Dominican Centennial of 1922.

Leaving St. Catharines, April 7, 1922.

❖
The Dominican Sisters in a procession at the time of their centennial on April 7, 1922.

The school of St. Louis Bertrand in Louisville was taught by the Dominican Sisters. Here Sister Agnes Marie Smith stands to the left, with Fr. Timothy Leonard Crowley to the right.

Students of St. Catharine Academy found themselves in an impressive conveyance in a photograph probably taken in the 1890's.

Ursuline College stood upon these grounds from 1938 until 1968. Today the campus on Lexington Road thrives with five schools.

Ursuline Sisters arrived in Louisville in 1858 from Straubing, Germany to begin the work of education. Ursuline Academy began at Shelby and Chestnut Streets in 1859. In 1877 a boarding school opened in the Lexington Road area named Sacred Heart Academy. In 1917 an impressive new Motherhouse opened on Lexington Road. The Motherhouse — Rotunda — Chapel was dedicated December 8, 1917 during the First World War. It was one of the coldest days on record in Louisville.

❖ **U**rsuline Motherhouse Chapel. Circa 1960.

❖ **U**rsuline Chapel on Chestnut Street about 1900.

Commercial class 1907-08.
Ursuline Academy.

Junior class 1905-06.
Ursuline Academy.

Freshman class 1905-06.
Ursuline Academy.

Intermediate grades - 1912.
Ursuline Academy.

7th/8th grades 1907-08.
Ursuline Academy.

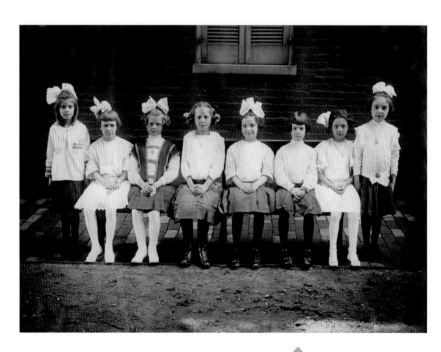

Primary grades 1912.
Ursuline Academy.

Class of 1901. Ursuline Academy.

Mount St. Joseph Academy was founded in Daviess County by five Ursuline Sisters from Louisville in 1874. By 1912, the flourishing community in that location near Owensboro was designated an autonomous motherhouse popularly known as Maple Mount. A Junior College begun on the grounds in 1925 moved to Owensboro in 1950 and now is known as Brescia University.

The convent chapel at Mount St. Joseph on August 10, 1915.

Sacred Heart statue on the Maple Mount grounds.

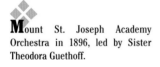 **A** youth orchestra at Mount St. Joseph. Date unknown. The original photographer managed to reverse the negative in processing.

Mount St. Joseph Academy Orchestra in 1896, led by Sister Theodora Guethoff.

First postulants of Mount St. Joseph. Aug. 15, 1895. Seated is Mother Aloysius Willett.

Sister Agnes O'Flynn, Mother Aloysius Willett and Sister Vincentia Spalding pose with graduates of Mount Saint Joseph Academy in 1913.

The Sisters of Divine Providence have served in Kentucky since their first American foundation was made at Newport in 1889. The educational and social works of the community grew rapidly as did vocations. The community acquired property at Melbourne in 1908, and there an impressive provincial center was to rise. Known as St. Anne's Convent, the buildings dominate the landscape around them today.

◆ **S**isters Mary Odilia and Mary Pankratia stepped from a train in Covington in 1874 to begin the work of the Sisters of Notre Dame in Kentucky. Among their other teaching duties, the growing community began Notre Dame Academy. In 1924 a provincialate of the sisters was established in Covington and a new major convent center was dedicated at St. Joseph Heights along Dixie Highway in 1927. The structure remains a major presence in the area.

◆ **S**ome members of the community in 1927.

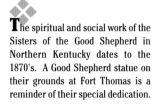The spiritual and social work of the Sisters of the Good Shepherd in Northern Kentucky dates to the 1870's. A Good Shepherd statue on their grounds at Fort Thomas is a reminder of their special dedication.

 group of the sisters in 1919.

German Benedictine sisters left Eichstätt in 1852 to begin their labors in America. From their convent in Erie, Pennsylvania, a group of three sisters came to Covington in 1859. Soon St. Walburg Academy was underway. And as early as 1867 a group of the sisters went to Ferdinand, Indiana to establish the community there that now is a landmark of that locality (see page 157). With the onset of the 20th century, the Covington community looked for room to expand and found a commanding location west of the city where an elegant Villa Madonna Academy building (above) was dedicated in 1907. The striking building with its cupola is still a regional landmark at the St. Walburg Monastery. Villa Madonna College would begin on these grounds in 1921. It would move to Covington as a diocesan college in 1929 and later move to Crestview Hills. It is now known as Thomas More College.

SISTERS

INDIANA

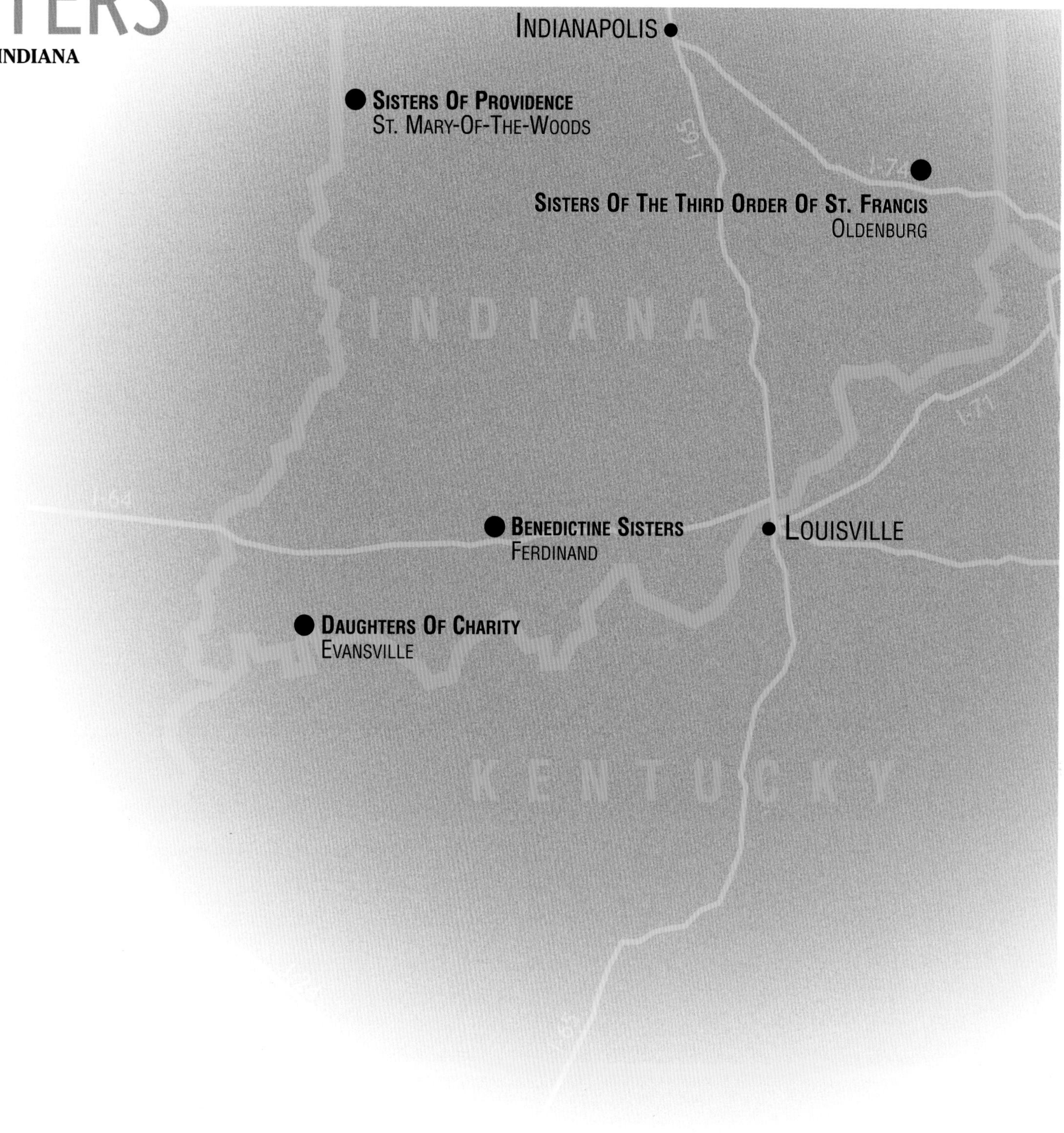
INDIANAPOLIS
SISTERS OF PROVIDENCE
ST. MARY-OF-THE-WOODS
I-74
SISTERS OF THE THIRD ORDER OF ST. FRANCIS
OLDENBURG
I-65
INDIANA
I-71
I-64
BENEDICTINE SISTERS
FERDINAND
LOUISVILLE
DAUGHTERS OF CHARITY
EVANSVILLE
KENTUCKY

EVANSVILLE
FERDINAND
OLDENBURG
PROVIDENCE

German-speaking Benedictine Sisters arrived in Ferdinand in 1867 to begin their educational mission. Construction of the massive and remarkable Church of the Immaculate Conception began here in 1915 and came to completion in 1924. The chief architect of the Romanesque structure atop Mount Tabor was Victor Klutho of St. Louis. Around the church are walkways and pagodas. The windows were designed by Fr. Bede Maier of St. Meinrad and completed by Frei Art Glass Studios.

❖ **T**he Cloister Hall at Ferdinand leads visitors to the community's distinctive church. Within, twenty-six windows portray noted Benedictine saints.

A view from the convent cemetery shows a rear view of the church. It also suggests why the Benedictine monastery is known as "The Castle on the Hill." The Romanesque dome rises eighty-seven feet from the sanctuary floor.

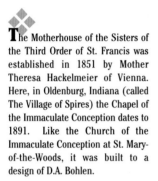

The Motherhouse of the Sisters of the Third Order of St. Francis was established in 1851 by Mother Theresa Hackelmeier of Vienna. Here, in Oldenburg, Indiana (called The Village of Spires) the Chapel of the Immaculate Conception dates to 1891. Like the Church of the Immaculate Conception at St. Mary-of-the-Woods, it was built to a design of D.A. Bohlen.

❖ The motherhouse cemetery is distinctive in noting on its stones both the baptismal and religious names of the deceased sisters.

❖ Whimsical painters have turned fire hydrants around the Oldenburg convent into folk-art with a Franciscan bent.

❖

Near Terre Haute, Indiana, stands the Motherhouse of the Sisters of Providence at St. Mary-of-the-Woods. Here are to be found a highly respected college and an immensely imposing church. This edifice began service in 1886 and is of Italian Renaissance design, modeled after the Church of the Holy Trinity in Paris. Diederich Bohlen of Indianapolis and his son Oscar were responsible for the design. Bohlen also designed the revered St. John Church in downtown Indianapolis.

Blessed
Mother Theodore Guerin
Foundress

Sisters of Providence
Saint Mary-of-the-Woods,
Indiana, USA

—LOUISVILLE—
THE BLESSED COMES TO CALL: 1840

In October, 1998, Pope John Paul II declared Mother Theodore Guerin to be Blessed. Such a beatification is often a step toward a declaration of sainthood.

Mother Theodore's feast day has been set as October 3. In 1840 this stalwart French religious arrived in the United States and made her way to Indiana to establish a motherhouse of the Sisters of Providence.

On her way inland from her ocean voyage, Mother Theodore passed through Louisville where she visited from October 2nd to 4th, 1840, thus spending the day that was to become her feast day in the Kentucky metropolis. While in the city, she met with Fr. Stephen Badin and stayed with the Sisters of Charity of Nazareth. This means she would have been with them on Fifth Street where they lived by St. Louis Church, which would be named the Cathedral within the year.

Mother Theodore Guerin kept a journal of her travels. By turning to its pages, we get a wonderful glimpse into Catholic life in Louisville at the beginning of the 1840's.

The following selection comes from **The Journals and Letters of Mother Theodore Guerin**, edited by Sister Mary Theodosia Mug (St. Mary of the Woods: Providence Press, 1937), pp.49-52.

REPRINTED WITH PERMISSION

❖❖❖

Continuing to descend the Ohio, we directed our course toward Louisville, Kentucky, which is forty-five miles from Madison. I wished to spend a day there in order to pay a visit to Reverend N. Perché, a missionary priest whom I knew at Angers and who was then living only about three miles from Louisville.

We reached the city in a few hours. As the boat was to stop there for some time, we went ashore to see the good Angerin. We were received by the Sisters of Charity, but a different community from those we had seen in the East. These were from Nazareth, under the direction of Bishop Flaget, in whose diocese we then were. Leaving my companions with these dear Sisters, and accompanied by Father Chartier and Sister Basilide, I went to Portland, the mission of Father Perché. He was away from home and was not to return till the following day; so we were deprived of the pleasure of seeing him.

At our return we had the honor of meeting the greatly esteemed Father Badin, that veteran among the missionaries, who for fifty years had exercised the functions of the ministry undertaken for the love of God and the salvation of his brethren. He was the first priest ordained in this country and, though he has suffered unheard-of trials and fatiguing labors, he still retains all his French gayety and joviality, if I may thus express myself. His stories provoked hearty laughter. His countenance expressed innocence, candor, and holiness; one feels better after seeing him. He remained a long time with us at the Sisters'. His enquiries about my traveling companions led to the discovery that one of the number, Sister Olympiade, is his cousin. We felt it a great honor to be related to this holy man.

The next morning, feast of the Angels, he heard our confessions. It was a sweet consolation to address ourselves to this venerable priest. It seemed that the words of divine truth had extraordinary strength coming from those lips which had been employed so long in teaching the truth and had effected so many wonders. He has indeed suffered for the faith. He now beholds forty priests in those parts that he alone evangelized for twenty years. During one period he was twenty-one months without seeing a Catholic priest, consequently, unable to have the benefit of sacramental confession.

This holy man, having heard our confessions and encouraged us, said Mass for us. Then he came to take breakfast at the good Sisters', who are admirable for their charity, not-withstanding their poverty which appears to me to be very great. They have nearly the same costume as the other American Sisters of Charity, except the head-dress. They wear a bonnet it can be called, consisting of a piece of pasteboard of at least a foot in diameter, to which a second piece is attached to form the front. Behind, there is a curtain of lustring attached to this bonnet and which falls down the middle of the back, like that worn by our "Vendéennes." Under this coarse exterior they hide very precious virtures and rare talents. The Superior possesses artistic talent in a high degree. She reproduces nature with an accuracy and dexterity that are truly remarkable. They also teach music; without this branch, again I say, no pupils, neither rich nor poor.

These Sisters have no boarders here; they could not provide their fare. They served us boiled potatoes, dried herrings, corn bread, and old butter; we understood that the salt-fish was extra in our honor. We were amply compensated for the absence of bodily comforts, however, by the extraordinary kindness we met with.

The American Catholics here have the spirit of the Christians of the primitive Church: great charity, the love of hospitality which St. Paul recommends so strongly to the faithful of his time, an ardent zeal for the cause of the Gospel, in fine, all the virtues of Fathers of the Faith. I met several ladies of the highest rank, who had nothing more at heart than to bring up their children for the service of the Altar and Religion.

Having spent a long time in conversation with our good countryman, Father Badin, speaking much of Orleans and all dear France, we bade farewell to this holy priest and to the good Sisters and went to our boat which was to start at 3 P.M. that day. At the dock we learned that we must wait yet another day. We did not leave till 10 A.M. This delay gave us the opportunity to examine the town a little. Louisville has sprung up, as it were by magic, in a few years only. It is pretty, the streets are regular, and the houses (built à la francaise) are quite elegant. I have seen nothing better except Philadelphia; which, however, is far superior. The happy location, its rapid growth, its commerce, give us reason to presume that it will, before long, become one of the principal cities of America.

The following day we were again on the beautiful Ohio. Soon after leaving Louisville we came to the rapids, over which no boats can possibly pass; a canal, therefore, has been constructed with locks which hold back the water by enormous gates. When the boat is in one of these locks the water in the other can be seen more than sixteen feet below. One would imagine that there is going to be a terrible fall down, and that the boat must perish. Not at all! One side of these lower gates is opened and the water precipitates itself forcibly into the inclosure; then, when it has risen to a level with that where the boat is, the other gates are opened and we enter the lock. This operation has to be gone through six times before we come to the river again, which here has resumed its tranquil appearance, and continues to carry upon its surface a great number of boats.

◆ **S**t. Anne with the child Mary.

◆ **S**t. Michael the Archangel.

The Blessed Sacrament Chapel at St. Mary-of-the-Woods opened in 1924. At its center it features the Host in a radiant monstrance situated among angelic figures. The baldachin altar was carved in its entirety from a single eight-thousand pound block of Carrara marble from Italy.

◆ Views at the cemetery of the community at St. Mary-of-the-Woods. On the right, in a scene from one of the sculptural Stations of the Cross, Simon of Cyrene is seen aiding Jesus in carrying the cross.

Night scene: Mater Dei (Mother of God) is the special Patroness of the Province.

Our Lady of Grace statue welcomes all to the provincial offices.

A statue of St. Elizabeth Ann Seton on the grounds.

❖❖❖

With congregational roots tracing back to St. Vincent de Paul, St. Louise de Marillac, and St. Elizabeth Ann Seton, the Daughters of Charity began their work in Indiana in 1838. Their special ministries of health, education, and social service expanded greatly with the years. A new province was established in 1969 and moved its provincialate to Evansville in 1971.

A log cabin chapel, a reminder of frontier days, was constructed on the foundation of a former structure on the grounds.

The Mater Dei Provincialate sits on 195 acres of land on the west side of Evansville on New Harmony Road.

An angel stands sentry in Louisville's St. Michael Cemetery
and memorializes the Poschinger family.

CEMETERIES

Few places evoke such crosscurrents of emotion for believers as the cemetery. Here are mingled sadness and tragedy, memory and serenity, faith and hope. Laden with memorials to an incredible spectrum of human stories and histories, cemeteries are marked with classical symbols of living and dying, believing and striving. In granite and marble and bronze those who remain behind have placed their memorials and tributes. These are truly places of benediction for both the living and the dead.

In the following pages we present images — and the occasional story — from these holy lands of the dead. These pictures are chosen from cemetery sites across Kentucky and southern Indiana. But as usual, with Louisville serving as a geographical home-base for this virtual pilgrimage, we take special note here of the four major archdiocesan cemeteries that spread across Louisville: St. John (opened 1851); St. Michael (1851); St. Louis (1867) and Calvary (1921). The first two named were initially primarily German burial sites. In fact, St. Michael's at first bore the additional title "Gottes-Acker" or God's Acre. St. Louis was initially thought of as the "Irish" cemetery, while Calvary began under the title "St. Louis Cemetery Number 2."

The first Catholic burial site in the city had been around the early St. Louis Church that stood near Tenth and Main from 1811 to 1830. It is believed that many of these graves were transferred to a Catholic section of the public cemetery along the south side of Jefferson Street between 14th and 16th Streets. Almost all of these in turn were believed to have been moved to St. Louis Cemetery after its opening in 1867. The name St. Louis almost certainly was derived from the name of the city church of St. Louis that was retitled as the Cathedral of the Assumption after 1849. Catholic cemetery officials estimate the total burials of Catholics within Jefferson County are now close to 140,000. That is almost exactly the estimated population of Catholics living in Jefferson County today.

CEMETERIES
LOUISVILLE

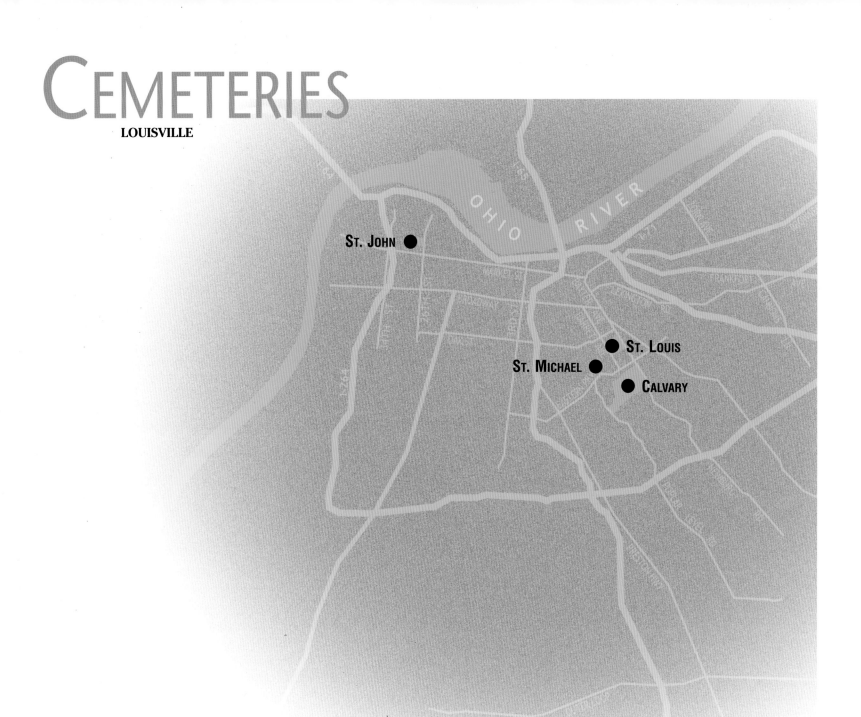

St. John ●

St. Louis ●

St. Michael ●

Calvary ●

OHIO RIVER

CALVARY
ST. JOHN
ST. LOUIS
ST. MICHAEL

**St**. Louis Cemetery on Barret Avenue offers dozens of statuesque angels.

Perry Doerhoefer was a young Louisvillian from a prominent family who died at 18 years of age on June 19, 1891. The cause of death was consumption, a common killer in that era. In St. Louis Cemetery he is represented life-sized and bearing the cross. Members of his family have kindly provided a photograph that may have been used as a model for the monument.

◆ **L**auber Family Memorial.

❤ **V**irgie Aileen Hocker Memorial.
Died August 17, 1890 – 3 years of age.

◆ **C**olonel Matt Winn is buried in St. Louis Cemetery. The man credited with making the Kentucky Derby an international event, Winn was buried from Louisville's Cathedral of the Assumption on October 8, 1949. Over his casket was spread a blanket of red roses, similar to that worn by Derby winners.

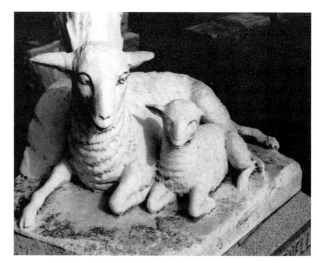

◆ **C**ornell Memorial.

◆ The Krieger twins — Chester and Arthur — were born September 15, 1887, two years after the end of the term of office of President Chester Arthur. Both boys had died before they reached the age of two. Vandalism has taken its toll over the years.

◆ Democratic Party leader "Mickey" Brennan.

◆ Joseph De Nunzio Monument. Here one of the city's earliest leading fruit merchants is shown leaning on a citrus crate.

◆ Even in death, Officer Charles McPeek is vigilant.

A young brother and sister stand serenely in stone at St. Louis Cemetery. The Doyle children — Gertrude Lilly, 6, and Henry Charles, 3, died within nine days of each other in a diptheria epidemic that afflicted the city in 1890. (Other near-by graves of children indicate similar death dates).

Gertrude Lilly, the last to die, was buried from home because fear of contagion prevented a church funeral. As she lay dying on January 12, 1890, "a bright Sunday afternoon," this scene unfolded, as later recorded in a family history written by her only surviving sibling, John Fredrick Doyle:

John A. [her father] then stepped to the bedside of his child. Her face lighted, she smiled and said "I see Jesus." That was the end. The devoted pastor of the Cathedral, Rev. Patrick Rock, said he truly believed the child had seen a vision.

❖❖❖

The writer of this account, John Frederick Doyle, was the father of Sister of Charity of Nazareth Mary Ellen Doyle, a researcher and writer, who kindly made the text and accompanying photograph available.

The Doyle children about 1889: John Frederick, Henry Charles and Gertrude Lilly. The latter two are memorialized in the poignant statue in St. Louis Cemetery. John Frederick, (on the left), was later to pen the account of his little sister's death. They were the children of Cathedral parish members John Philip Augustine (known as John A.) Doyle and Agnes Frances Harig Doyle.

Little Jennie Judge (1861-1865) lived a very brief life, its dates the same as the American Civil War. Also buried on this plot is Maggie Judge Hutchins (1860-1941) a hearing-impaired woman who became a significant force in civic life and at the Cathedral of the Assumption.

PRIEST CIRCLE

The coat of arms of Louisville's Bishop Denis O'Donaghue (1910-1924 in office) at St. Louis Cemetery.

SISTERS OF MERCY

LITTLE SISTERS OF THE POOR

◆ Many of the Little Sisters of the Poor — who first arrived in Louisville in 1869 — are buried in St. Louis Cemetery.

◆ Graves of the Sisters of Mercy — who also arrived in Louisville in 1869.

XAVERIAN BROTHERS

❖ **T**he Xaverian Brothers from Belgium made their first American foundation at Louisville in 1854. Ten years later they opened the institution now known as St. Xavier High School. Many of the Xaverian Brothers are buried in Louisville's St. Louis Cemetery.

The body of Louisville-born Victor Mature (1913-1999) now rests in St. Michael Cemetery. The Mourning Angel monument to the Hollywood star and his family was crafted in Italy.

FRANCISCAN FRIARS

On Thursday, April 28, 1881, a sudden thunderstorm struck as several boys from St. Anthony School near 23rd and Market Streets played baseball. A sudden bolt of lightning took the lives of four of the youths: Leo Fleck, Wilhelm Pfalzer, Frank Schneider and George Schulte. Young Pfalzer, who was at bat when the lightning struck, is buried beneath this eroding stone at St. Michael Cemetery, near the Texas Avenue entrance. A Louisville physician interviewed by **The Louisville Commercial** just after the tragedy was of the opinion that the unusual display of lightning resulted from "conjunctive planets."

The German presence is very strong in St. Michael Cemetery.

The burial plot of Franciscan Friars.

SISTERS OF THE GOOD SHEPHERD

◆ **F**ive Sisters of the Good Shepherd — representing five nationalities — settled in Louisville in 1843 at the invitation of Bishop Flaget. The Good Shepherd Sisters remain an active presence in Louisville today. Deceased members of the community are buried in Calvary Cemetery.

◆ **D**eMarsh Family Memorial.

◆ **S**t. Joseph and Christ Child. Pezzullo Family Memorial.

◆ **S**everal of the religious communities that have served faithfully for well over a century are buried in Louisville Catholic cemeteries.

The Confederate guerrilla William Clarke Quantrill (1835-65) was captured and taken to Louisville in May, 1865. While imprisoned, he converted to Catholicism. After his death on June 6, 1865, he was buried for a time in St. John Cemetery, but the body was later moved.

IN MEMORY OF
REV. C. J.
BOESWALD
BORN
FEB. 27, 1802
ORDAINED
NOV. 5, 1843
DIED
NOV. 5, 1855
FIRST CHAPLAIN OF
ST. JOSEPH'S
ORPHAN HOME

The gravestone of Fr. Charles Joseph Boeswald in St. John Cemetery. A native of Germany and a zealous priest, he was wounded by a mob during the Bloody Monday Riots of August, 1855. He was stricken with typhoid that same autumn and died soon thereafter, on the twelfth anniversary of his ordination.

Moran Family Memorial.

CEMETERIES
KENTUCKY HOLY LAND

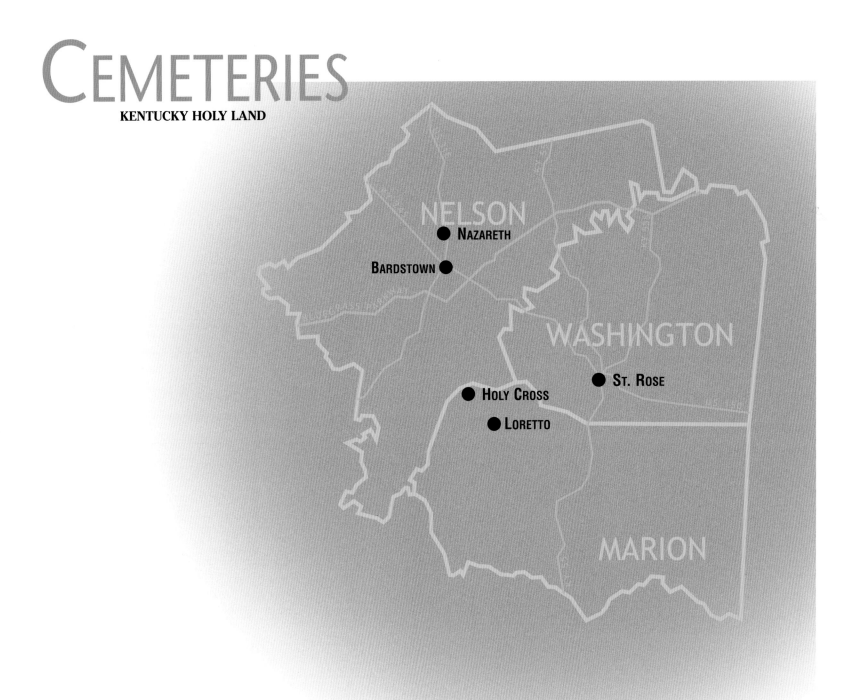

NELSON

● Nazareth

Bardstown ●

WASHINGTON

● Holy Cross

● St. Rose

● Loretto

MARION

BARDSTOWN
HOLY CROSS
LORETTO
NAZARETH
ST. ROSE

Sister Ann Spalding was the sister of Mother Catherine Spalding, first superior of the Sisters of Charity of Nazareth. Sister Ann was in charge of St. Catherine Academy at Lexington and there she met a tragic and untimely end. According to the centennial history of St. Catherine's: "The sisters had some women slaves working about the house. Sister Ann unwittingly offended one of these slaves and was poisoned by her." The fatal dosage was placed inside buttermilk. "The sisters had the young slave girl sent south, but had nothing further done to her." Sister Ann Spalding died May 15, 1848.

In the Nazareth Motherhouse Cemetery stands the grave of Sister Catherine Malone who died while serving as a volunteer Civil War nurse in Louisville.

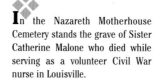

Fr. Eugene Angelo Bertello died in the train accident at Shepherdsville in Christmas week 1917. He was one of over forty killed on a train that had come from Louisville. Pious legend maintained that he was carrying the Eucharist to a sick parishioner.

Three Mrs. Alexander Hamiltons in the cemetery at St. Rose in Washington County.

Sacred Heart of Jesus. Bardstown Catholic Cemetery.

Lancaster Memorial. Bardstown Catholic Cemetery.

Cissell Memorial. Holy Cross Cemetery.

A collection of broken stones. Holy Cross Cemetery.

The grave of Fr. Athanasius A. Aud at the Loretto Motherhouse Cemetery.

Fr. John Hutchins Memorial. Loretto Motherhouse Cemetery.

The memorial to Fr. David Deparcq at the Loretto Motherhouse Cemetery.

The first priest to die in Kentucky was Anthony Salmon, a Frenchman, who died in a fall from his horse while he performed his duties, though weakened by illness. He died November 10, 1799, and is buried at Holy Cross. His broken stone bearing a Latin inscription notes that he chose exile to "schismatic wealth."

At the Loretto Motherhouse Cemetery, the monument to Fr. Francis Wuyts is in Latin. The translation reads, in part: *I was Belgian. Now I am not. I am a citizen and resident of death...place your hope in the Lord...*

Sister Jean Connor, age 29, volunteered for nursing service at Louisville's Camp Zachary Taylor during the deadly influenza epidemic that spread across America near the end of the First World War. Stricken herself by the disease, she died in the city October 28, 1918. After a military funeral at Camp Taylor, she was buried at the Loretto Motherhouse Cemetery. An old photo reportedly shows her shortly before her entry into the Sisters of Loretto.

An angelic crown awaits Fr. Augustine Degauquier (1802-1870) on his tombstone at the Loretto Motherhouse Cemetery.

CEMETERIES

KENTUCKY

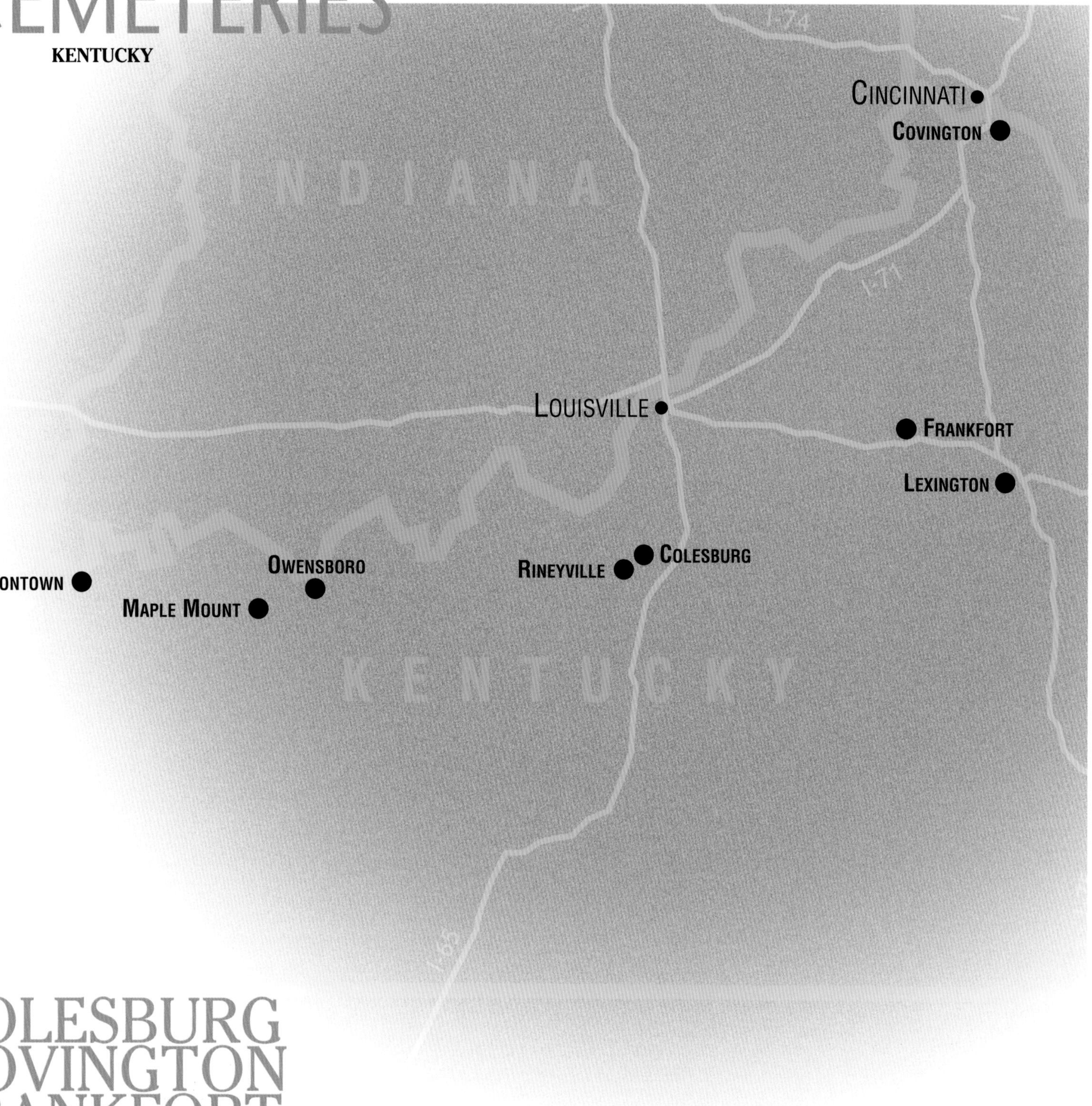

CINCINNATI ●

COVINGTON ●

LOUISVILLE ●

FRANKFORT ●

LEXINGTON ●

OWENSBORO ●

COLESBURG ●

RINEYVILLE ●

UNIONTOWN ●

MAPLE MOUNT ●

COLESBURG
COVINGTON
FRANKFORT
LEXINGTON
MAPLE MOUNT
OWENSBORO
RINEYVILLE
UNIONTOWN

❖ "**H**e is risen. He is not here." So reads the biblical message borne by an angel on the monument to famed artist Frank Duveneck (1848-1919). He is buried in Mother of God Cemetery in Kenton County.

❖ **A** Crucifixion Group is a common central memorial to all the deceased in many burial grounds across Kentucky and Indiana. This sculpture stands at Covington's Mother of God Cemetery.

Deceased children of the Howard Family in Owensboro's Mater Dolorosa Cemetery.

Moving memorials to young children in Lexington's Calvary Cemetery.

St. John Cemetery at Rineyville. Burials began here early in the 19th century.

Two young Confederate soldiers from Curdsville in western Kentucky were captured while their company was recruiting in Daviess County. The two ran afoul of an order issued by U.S. General Stephen Burbridge ordering retaliation executions for a recent attempt on the life of a prominent citizen of Henderson. Soldiers Charles Thompson and Pierman Powell were taken to Henderson and shot by the river in that city July 22, 1864. Both Catholic, they asked for and received rosaries as they were about to meet their deaths. They are buried at St. Alphonsus Parish Cemetery near the Maple Mount Motherhouse. Their friends are said to have placed the C.S.A. initials (Confederate States of America) after the Burbridge name as their own form of retaliation against the staunchly Unionist Burbridge.

St. Clare Cemetery. Colesburg.

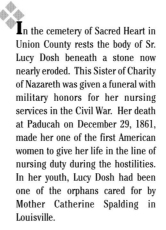 In the cemetery of Sacred Heart in Union County rests the body of Sr. Lucy Dosh beneath a stone now nearly eroded. This Sister of Charity of Nazareth was given a funeral with military honors for her nursing services in the Civil War. Her death at Paducah on December 29, 1861, made her one of the first American women to give her life in the line of nursing duty during the hostilities. In her youth, Lucy Dosh had been one of the orphans cared for by Mother Catherine Spalding in Louisville.

The memorial stone of Fr. Thomas Major, pastor of Good Shepherd Church in Kentucky's state capital, is to be found in Frankfort Cemetery. Before becoming a Catholic and a priest, Major had a colorful career. He enlisted with Confederate forces during the Civil War, serving with John Hunt Morgan. He was captured by the Union and escaped by digging a tunnel. He owed his conversion, he said, to a nun who was his nurse in a Civil War military hospital.

At Sacred Heart Cemetery near Uniontown in Union County.

CEMETERIES

INDIANA

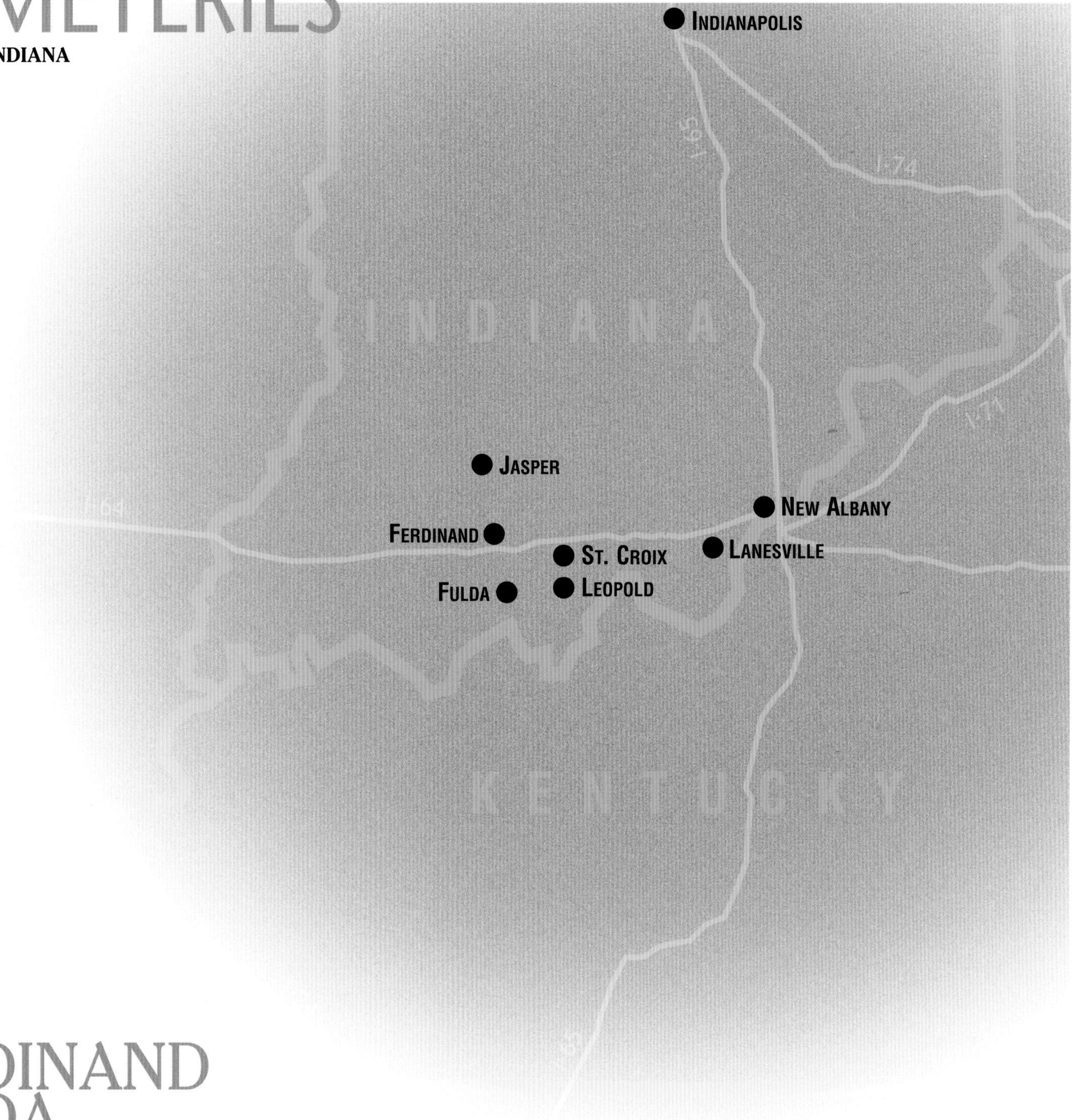

● INDIANAPOLIS

I N D I A N A

● JASPER

● NEW ALBANY

FERDINAND ●

● ST. CROIX ● LANESVILLE

FULDA ● ● LEOPOLD

K E N T U C K Y

FERDINAND
FULDA
INDIANAPOLIS
JASPER
LANESVILLE
LEOPOLD
NEW ALBANY
ST. CROIX

One of several French inscriptions to be found in the parish burial grounds of Leopold.

Angel at Jasper.

A young veteran of the Second World War at St. Croix.

Another young Indiana veteran of the Second World War. St. Boniface Church Yard at Fulda.

An infant's grave at St. Croix.

At St. Mary Church at Lanesville.

A grave marker at St. Ferdinand Parish for soldier Samuel Fitter who died — most likely of influenza — in the last days of the First World War.

The Benedictine Sisters burial grounds at Ferdinand.

❖ **A**t Holy Trinity in New Albany, the grave of Supreme Court Justice Sherman Minton (1890-1965), a convert to Catholicism. A bridge bearing his name links New Albany and Louisville.

❖ **V**ery frequently — as here at Holy Trinity Cemetery in New Albany — the bereaved Irish caused the name of the home county in the Old Country to be carved onto the stone of their beloved.

❖ **T**he founding pastor of Holy Trinity congregation in New Albany, Indiana is commemorated by a plaque in the parish cemetery. Fr. Neyron had been at Waterloo with Napoleon, prior to his clerical studies, and would later teach at the University of Notre Dame.

REV. J.M. VILLARS
NATIVE OF CHAVANAY
DEPT. OF LOIRE, FRANCE
DIED RICHMOND, IND.
MARCH 5. 1868
AGE 50 YRS

Special Dispatch to the Indianapolis Journal.

A CATHOLIC PRIEST HANGS HIMSELF AT RICHMOND, INDIANA.

RICHMOND, IND., March 6.

At a late hour this morning Rev. J. M. Voilor, pastor of St. Mary's Catholic church, of this city, was found dead in his room. During the night he hanged himself with a large silk neck tie, attached to a part of his bed. He was quite an old man, and was in poor health, which is supposed to have caused him to take his life.

◆ An 1868 item in **The Indianapolis Journal**.

◆◆
The unusual case of Fr. John Villars leads us to stray slightly north of the geographical range of these pages. The French priest was pastor at Richmond, Indiana, where he was found dead from hanging on March 5, 1868. While the immediate fear was suicide, subsequently a strong conviction arose that he had been murdered. He was buried at St. Joseph Cemetery on the south side of Indianapolis. There his tomb has become a place over the years where visitors leave written prayers and occasionally coins on the grave.

Window detail from the Cathedral
Basilica of the Assumption, Covington.

ART GLASS

THE RADIANCE OF GLASS

One of the artistic glories of Medieval Christendom was the fashioning of art in glass usually associated with great cathedrals and monastic churches. That tradition, of course, continues down into our own time. The radiant art of glass in the religious context renders visible a dazzling magnitude of diverse images and experiences, usually drawn from the scriptures and church history.

Especially in America, as construction technologies as well as parish finances improved in the nineteenth and early twentieth centuries, parish and cathedral churches seemed to outdo one another to make their mark in colorful glass. As heirs of that tradition, we still have among us in this part of the country a visual wealth of religious art in glass. Included here is a mere sampling. These gems must, of course, be seen in their own full settings to convey the majesty and awe so often intended by their original designers and crafters.

❖ St. Patrick as shown in a window at the Louisville Cathedral of the Assumption.

❖ St. Louis IX, King of France. This window at Louisville's Cathedral of the Assumption is a reference to the city's French heritage, and shows the saint holding the relic of Christ's Crown of Thorns. The window was first placed in the church in 1912, shortly after the sinking of the Titanic. It has now been restored and placed in the Blessed Sacrament Chapel of the Cathedral.

❖ The stained glass entry to Louisville's oldest continuously operated school: Presentation Academy staffed by the Sisters of Charity of Nazareth since 1831. This building on Fourth Street dates to the 1890's.

For the central window at old St. Charles Church on Louisville's Chestnut Street (no longer serving as a Catholic sanctuary), the parish had a painting of St. Charles Borromeo in the Cathedral collection copied in glass — but with modifications. St. Charles, for example, envisions in the right distance the Louisville church that will bear his name.

The Good Shepherd as portrayed at old St. Charles.

At the Chapel at the Dominican Sisters Motherhouse near Springfield.

An angel at Holy Name Church in Henderson.

The fragile but safe ship on stormy seas in glass at St. Catharine Church in New Haven, Kentucky.

At St. Patrick Church, Maysville.

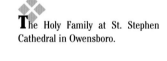

A majestic Christ at St. Stephen Cathedral.

The Holy Family at St. Stephen Cathedral in Owensboro.

Christ on the way to the Cross encounters St. John and the Blessed Virgin Mary (above). An angel (right) at St. Stephen Cathedral in Owensboro.

Stunning windows are found in the Mildred Stout Field Stained Glass Gallery at the Owensboro Museum of Fine Art. There on permanent display are sixteen windows saved from the demolished Catholic Church of St. Joseph, originally a German parish in Owensboro.

ST. HENRY II, STAINED GLASS, TURN-OF-THE-CENTURY, MUNICH, GERMANY, EMIL FREI (1867-1941), COLLECTION OF OWENSBORO MUSEUM OF FINE ART, KY. A GIFT OF THE ROMAN CATHOLIC DIOCESE OF OWENSBORO.

ST. HUBERTUS, STAINED GLASS, TURN-OF-THE-CENTURY, MUNICH, GERMANY, EMIL FREI (1867-1941), COLLECTION OF OWENSBORO MUSEUM OF FINE ART, KY. A GIFT OF THE ROMAN CATHOLIC DIOCESE OF OWENSBORO.

❖ The pelican on glass at Nazareth is drawn from an emblem of the Sisters of Charity. In medieval legend, the pelican took from its own body to feed its young and thus was a sign of selfless giving.

❖ St. Joseph, the Christ Child and a musical angel at the Motherhouse Church at Nazareth.

From the windows of St. Ann Church in Morganfield.

The Crucified Christ with St. Thomas Aquinas in the Church of St. Rose in Washington County near Springfield.

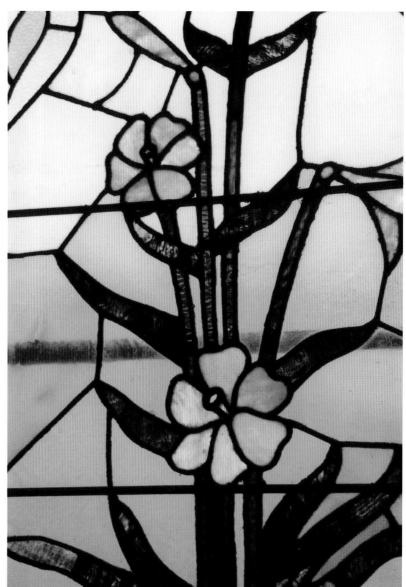

Distinctive floral windows appear at St. Bartholomew Church in Columbus, Indiana.

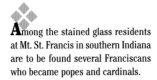

Among the stained glass residents at Mt. St. Francis in southern Indiana are to be found several Franciscans who became popes and cardinals.

Jesus the Good Shepherd at the Church at St. Mary-of-the-Woods.

Saints in glass at the Archabbey Church at St. Meinrad: St. Leo the Great, St. Ignatius Loyola and St. Stephen (detail below).

West Wall: The Good Shepherd.

West Wall Angel: I am the Way.

West Wall Angel: The Truth and the Life.

West Wall: St. Stephen.

❖❖❖

Like most of the great cathedrals of Europe (and the Cathedral in Louisville as well) the Archabbey Church was constructed so that worshippers would face east (toward Jerusalem / The Resurrection / the Rising Sun) upon entering. The west wall has particularly striking windows that become radiant with the setting sun. These were crafted by the Emil Frei Studio of St. Louis, and contain, among others, depictions of Christ the Good Shepherd, St. Stephen Martyr, and angels bearing scrolls.

St. Bernard of Clairvaux on canvas in the
collection of the Cathedral of the Assumption
in Louisville.

SITES AND SCENES

Throughout this area there stands quite an array of evidence of faith-in-action, faith-in-institutional form, and faith as expressed in the visual arts. Churches are usually the repositories of such expressions, but the museum, the wayside shrine, the school, and other sites can give evidence as well to the long Catholic involvement with the historical, the sacramental and the beautiful. The pages of this chapter can only point to a few representative images in a region blessed with their abundance.

Also included here are several old "roll" photographs made at special parish events. This long serial shot was especially in use in the years from about 1910 to 1950. After that year, they rarely surface in local archival sources.

The missionary priests and bishops of Kentucky in the first half of

the 19th century were accustomed to go begging in Europe – both

for funds as well as for art work for their remote diocese. Most of

these art works remain in Kentucky today, especially at the

Cathedral in Louisville and at the Proto-Cathedral in Bardstown. At

least two kings (Ferdinand II of The Two Sicilies and Ludwig I of

Bavaria) and one pope (Gregory XVI) were among the donors.

One of the best known paintings in the collection of the Cathedral in Louisville is believed to have come from the brush of Antwerp's 17th century painter Gaspar de Crayer, although it was at one time attributed to Rubens. The painting shows the dramatic scene when St. Bernard of Clairvaux (1090-1153) approaches William, Duke of Aquitaine with the Host. The Duke had been described as "haughty...with a violent temper" and Bernard is said to come before him in a benevolent confrontation.

Legend says that the Duke embraced humility and changed his ways. Thus the canvas can be seen as an allegory of the transforming power of the Eucharist. *(Above: detail of the Duke. A detail of St. Bernard appears on page 218.)*

Bishop Martin John Spalding (1810-1872) - by George Healy (1865) at Bardstown Historical Museum.

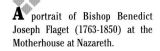

A portrait of Bishop Benedict Joseph Flaget (1763-1850) at the Motherhouse at Nazareth.

St. Vincent de Paul with orphans – and a Sister of Charity of Nazareth looking on. This creative use of chronology (St. Vincent died in 1660 and the S.C.N.'s were founded in 1812) was incorporated into this painting by J. Krementz in the 1870's. The canvas is located in the Archives of the Archdiocese of Louisville.

❖ Chasuble (Mass Vestment) believed to have belonged to Bishop Benedict Joseph Flaget. A radiant Agnus Dei (Lamb of God) is at the center. It is located at the Archives of the Archdiocese of Louisville.

❖ Rare volumes from the Special Collections of the Spalding University Library.

❖ Chant book in the Special Collections of the Spalding University Library.

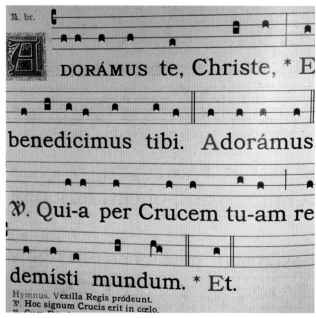

❖ Missal from Gethsemani at the Bardstown Historical Museum.

THE SPEED ART MUSEUM IN LOUISVILLE POSSESSES A SUPERB COLLECTION OF RELIGIOUS ART. TO BE FOUND AMONG ITS TREASURES ARE THESE:

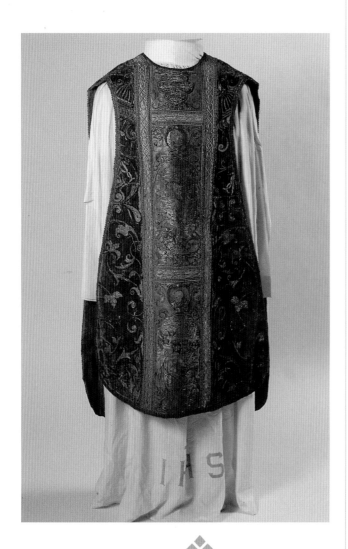

❖ **C**hasuble, late 16th century. Spanish.
COLLECTION OF THE SPEED ART MUSEUM, LOUISVILLE, KENTUCKY.

❖ **T**he Hierarchy of the Church, c. 1626. Peter Paul Rubens, Flemish 1577-1640. Oil on panel.
COLLECTION OF THE SPEED ART MUSEUM, LOUISVILLE, KENTUCKY.

❖ **C**halice, 1720. Gotthard Unterhuber, German, Vienna, Austria, 1688-1728. Gilded silver and gem stones.
COLLECTION OF THE SPEED ART MUSEUM, LOUISVILLE, KENTUCKY.

Reliquary, about 1850-1880 (based on late medieval models). Gilded copper.
COLLECTION OF THE SPEED ART MUSEUM, LOUISVILLE, KENTUCKY.

The Adoration of the Magi, 14th century. Ivory. French, Paris.
COLLECTION OF THE SPEED ART MUSEUM, LOUISVILLE, KENTUCKY.

OF THE MYRIAD OF NON-PAROCHIAL STRUCTURES IN THE REGION, WE PRESENT A SMALL HISTORICAL SAMPLING.

Louisville's Holy Cross High School (opened 1984) represents a merger of two post-World War II schools: Angela Merici and Bishop David. Other secondary schools in Louisville from that post-war era are Assumption (1955); DeSales (1956); and Trinity (1953).

Although these pages focus on older structures and institutions, the Holy Cross archway is shown here since it seems so carefully modeled on the gateway to Holy Cross, the historic church in the Kentucky Holy Land (p. 69).

Presentation Academy, dating to a foundation by Mother Catherine Spalding in 1831, is Louisville's oldest academy in continuous use. Its present main building was opened in 1895 at Fourth and Breckinridge Streets. Several other current Catholic secondary schools began in Louisville in the nineteenth century: St. Xavier (1864); Sacred Heart Academy (1877); Holy Rosary Academy (1867); and Mercy Academy (1885). Bethlehem High School in Bardstown, now in more recent facilities, traces its roots to 1819.

Spalding University represents an educational tradition of the Sisters of Charity of Nazareth dating back to 1814. Opened in Louisville in 1920 as Nazareth College, Spalding added this Academic Gothic building to its campus in 1942.

The Mansion at Spalding is an elegant late Victorian mansion on South Fourth Street that has been incorporated among newer structures. This side view shows the south side of the old residence.

Of the many Catholic health and social-service institutions that began in 19th century Louisville, few have maintained their Victorian era buildings. One such structure that has survived is St. Joseph Children's Home on Frankfort Avenue. This view from a golden anniversary book of 1899 reveals a time when the eastern side of the city was decidedly rural in appearance.

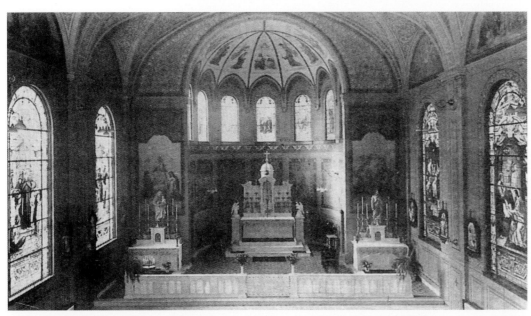

The structure now used by Kindred Hospital in Louisville was once that of St. Anthony Hospital, opened by Franciscan Sisters in 1900. The ornate chapel from 1915 is seen as it looked at the time of its opening. It is still in use.

The Mayo Mansion in Paintsville, Kentucky, in Johnson County, was completed in 1912 by coal baron John C. C. Mayo. The Greek Revival structure is now home to Our Lady of the Mountain parochial school.

Parish schools can at times reveal an architectural elegance as at St. Francis of Assisi Parish on Louisville's Bardstown Road. When this structure opened it was planned for educational purposes, though it served as a time as a temporary church as well. When the building was dedicated July 4, 1926, guest preacher Monsignor George Schuhmann reminded his hearers it was the 150th anniversary of American independence, and noted that the political thought of St. Robert Bellarmine may well have influenced Thomas Jefferson's ideas.

The Louisville Cathedral school building opened in 1867. It now houses Cathedral parish offices.

In Bardstown, Spalding Hall — now the home of the Oscar Getz Museum of Whiskey History and the Bardstown Historical Museum — stands as an historic building that once housed St. Joseph's College. It was begun in 1820 and completed in 1826. The school began life in 1820 as a diocesan institution and was later (after 1848) staffed by the Jesuit Fathers. During the Civil War, St. Joseph closed but the building served as a military hospital. The college re-opened in 1869 and continued in operation until 1889. The Xaverian Brothers ran a school there known as St. Joseph Preparatory ("St. Joe Prep") until 1968. Old Flaget High School in Louisville's West End is believed to have derived some of its architectural style from this building. St. Catharine College in Springfield now offers some classes in this structure.

❖
Old Flaget High School in Louisville's West End closed in 1974 and now houses apartments. Built in 1949, the building has a striking resemblance to Spalding Hall in Bardstown.

❖❖❖

ECHOES — This is but one more example of Louisville urban places that echo sites resonant in Catholic history. See, for example, Holy Spirit Church (p. 43); the Callahan home (p. 246); and the Holy Cross arch (p. 225). In an earlier era, Catholics at St. Thomas Farm in Nelson County built their church in 1816 to suggest the Paca Street Chapel in Baltimore, Maryland.

❖
This famed log house at St. Thomas Farm near Bardstown was the primal structure of St. Thomas Seminary, the first Catholic institution of its type in the West. Begun in 1795, this building was home to much of the work of such frontier Catholic leaders as Bishops Benedict Joseph Flaget and John Baptist David.

Flaget Hall at St. Joseph Proto-Cathedral in Bardstown once was used by the Jesuit Fathers at St. Joseph College. It was built in 1852 and now houses offices of the parish.

Now an apartment building in Louisville's Portland neighborhood, this structure once served as a school conducted by the Sisters of Loretto, beginning in 1842. Known as Mount St. Benedict, it was popularly called Cedar Grove. The school closed in 1925 but re-opened as Loretto Academy in the old Doerhoefer Mansion at Broadway and 45th Street. That institution closed in 1973. Here is shown a 19th century sketch of the building in a German history.

Cardome, now a community center in Georgetown, Kentucky, was the home of the Sisters of the Visitation from 1896 to 1987. A central feature of the property was an 1821 mansion. Here is the Visitation Academy graduating class of 1944 on the scenic grounds.

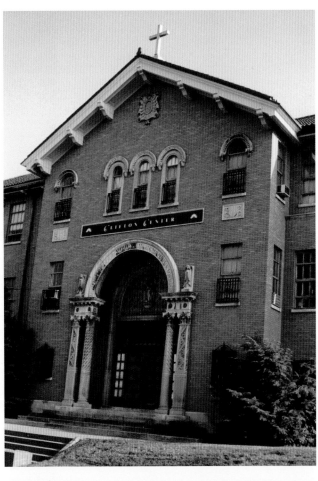

Another example of a school that was constructed with an eye to excellence in architectural design is that of St. Frances of Rome on Louisville's Payne Street. Opened c.1930, the building was designed by Nolan and Nolan. It was structured largely of concrete and now serves the community as the Clifton Center.

St. Vincent Academy was long a landmark in Union County, Kentucky, where pioneering Sisters of Charity of Nazareth arrived in 1820. The school closed in 1967, but its Victorian tower remains nearby today.

❖ In the parish church of St. Augustine at Leopold, Indiana, stands the Shrine of Our Lady of Consolation. The fascinating story of how this shrine came to be in southern Indiana takes us to one of the most horrific sites associated with the American Civil War: Andersonville Prison in Georgia. Among the prisoners in that notorious place were three young Union soldiers from Perry County, Indiana: Lambert Rogier, Henry Devillez and Isidore Naivaux. In their supplications to the Blessed Virgin Mary in their plight, they pledged that if they survived, they would arrange to have a statue of the Virgin placed at St. Augustine Church.

These young men were Belgian and they were mindful of the Shrine of Our Lady of Consolation in the Duchy of Luxembourg. It was a replica of the statue there that they vowed to have placed in Indiana. The three found release from Andersonville after eleven months of imprisonment. Lambert Rogier made the trip to Europe, acquired a copy of the statue, and arrived back in the Port of New York on July 4, 1867. From there it was transported to Leopold. Thus is a particular devotion that began in the 17th century still part of the life and piety of many in Indiana to this day.

❖ At historic New Harmony in southwest Indiana stands a medieval statue of the Madonna and Child imported from France. This wayside shrine is a memorial in honor of Trappist monk Thomas Merton.

❖ Often named as "the smallest chapel in the world," Monte Casino, built between 1901 and 1905, stands on the campus of Thomas More College at Covington, Kentucky. The chapel was moved here in 1965 from its original site on the grounds of a small, short-lived Benedictine monastic community in Covington in the late 19th century.

❖ One of the smallest chapels ever built in the region is this one, constructed in 1943 by Italian prisoners-of-war at Camp Atterbury near Columbus, Indiana.

❖❖
A landmark and river-emblem is the Christ of the Ohio statue that stands high above the Ohio at Troy, Indiana. Designed by Herbert Jogerst, a German sculptor and American prisoner-of-war from the Second World War, the statue and its base stand nineteen feet high. The figure was sculpted at St. Meinrad Archabbey and blessed by Archbishop Paul Schulte of Indianapolis, May 1, 1957.

AVE MARIA

Kính mừng Maria đầy
ơn phúc, Đức Chúa Trời
ở cùng Bà, Bà có phúc
lạ hơn mọi người nữ,
và Giêsu con lòng Bà
gồm phúc lạ.

Thánh Maria Đức Mẹ
Chúa Trời, cầu cho chúng
con là kẻ có tội, khi này
và trong giờ lâm tử.
Amen.

The most recent shrine to be built in Louisville honors an 18th century apparition of the Virgin Mary in Vietnam. Our Lady of La-Vang, at St. John Vianney Church in Louisville's South End, is also a tribute to the significant number of Vietnamese Catholics who have moved to this area. At the base of the shrine, the Ave Maria (Hail Mary) appears in twelve languages.

On February 4, 1940, Colonel Patrick Henry Callahan died at his home, 2800 Lexington Road in Louisville. The structure was modeled after Homewood in Baltimore, built by Charles Carroll, Catholic signer of the Declaration of Independence. This architectural reminder of the Maryland Catholic tradition was appropriate for Colonel Callahan who was so prominent a national lay Catholic leader in America in his era. Once a baseball player, he became a major industrialist and leader in the fields of enhanced inter-faith and inter-racial relations. He was named to the Order of St. Gregory by Pope Pius XI and was buried from the Cathedral. The house is now the presidential residence of the Southern Baptist Theological Seminary.

It is a bit far afield, but Kentuckian Abraham Lincoln (right) is to be found pictured with Archbishop John Hughes of New York (left) in the Cathedral of the Immaculate Conception in Springfield, Illinois.

A stone labyrinth — based on a pattern of one on the floor of Chartres Cathedral in France — spreads across a gentle roll of land in Daviess County, Kentucky. The pilgrim path, some sixty feet wide, was built by Clarice O'Bryan near Sorgho, outside Owensboro. Another well-known labyrinth is to be found at New Harmony in Indiana.

The school orchestra at St. Catherine Academy in Lexington about 1924. Staffed by the Sisters of Charity of Nazareth, St. Catherine began in Scott County in 1823; it moved to Lexington in the middle 1830's, and was in operation until 1951, and the opening of Lexington Catholic High School.

The Raywick Band about 1905.

A gathering of the Knights of St. Joseph in Louisville. Date and location uncertain. Probably about 1920.

Golden Jubilee of Sister M. Cyrilla. St. Martin Church, Louisville. 1923.

Golden Jubilee Rev. Charles P. Raffo. St. Charles Church, Louisville. 1934.

Silver Jubilee Rev. Bernard Ignatius Doherty. 1927.

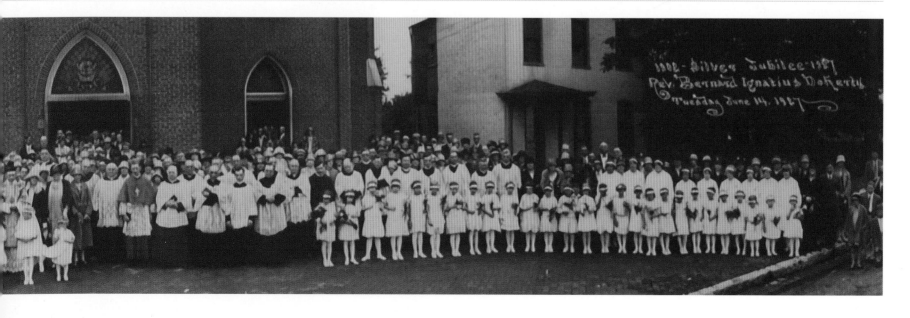

❖ **A** Holy Name Society gathering. Holy Rosary Parish, Springfield, Ky. About 1935.

❖ **C**atholic school children with plenty of pennants. Date and place uncertain.

❖ **1**911-1912 graduates of the Academy of Our Lady of Mercy, Louisville with Sisters of Mercy Mary Agnes McCarthy and Mary Bernardine Jarboe.

The 1927 Track Team of Louisville's St. Xavier High School with their coach, Brother Sylvanus.

First Communion Studio Photograph. Louisville. Date unknown.

❖ St. Boniface Church, Louisville. 1937.

❖ Baseball team at St. Joseph Parish in Louisville. 1916.

❖ The Sisters of Mercy began their work in Louisville in 1869. At Mercy Academy on East Broadway (founded in 1885) one finds today a statue that honors the community's foundress Catherine McAuley.

❖ Elizabeth (Sister Mary Winifred) Stevens, a Sister of Mercy. She grew up in St. Patrick Parish in Louisville and entered the convent in 1906.

❖ Her sister Nell in 1914.

❖ Date unknown.

A VARIETY OF SIGNS — SOME SOLEMN, SOME NOT — ARE TO BE FOUND

THROUGHOUT THE REGION.

A highway sign in Kentucky's Holy Land.

In Marion County, Kentucky.

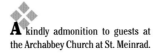

A kindly admonition to guests at the Archabbey Church at St. Meinrad.

A parking-ban is proclaimed at the Ursuline Motherhouse in Louisville.

A Latin inscription wishing peace to those who enter in the Rector's office at St. Meinrad School of Theology.

B ishop Benedict Joseph Flaget memorialized at Bardstown.

BENEDICT JOSEPH FLAGET
(1763-1850)

A priest for 62 years, the "First Bishop of the West" became Bishop of Bardstown, 1810; of Louisville, 1841. Jurisdiction embraced area of Ky., Tenn., and old Northwest Territory. Flaget directed founding of colleges, congregations, and St. Joseph's Cathedral; witnessed ten dioceses formed from region. Bishop buried in Louisville.

MARTIN JOHN SPALDING
Born May 23, 1810, near Calvary on the banks of the Rolling Fork. Graduated St. Mary's College, 1826. Ordained in 1834 at Urban College, Rome. Christian education and charity were his main interests. Established St. Vincent de Paul Society in 1854, for Christian charity. Appointed by the Pope as Archbishop of Baltimore in 1864. He died at Baltimore, Feb. 7, 1872.

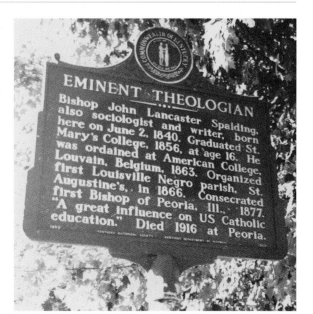

EMINENT THEOLOGIAN
Bishop John Lancaster Spalding, also sociologist and writer, born here on June 2, 1840. Graduated St. Mary's College, 1856, at age 16. He was ordained at American College, Louvain, Belgium, 1863. Organized first Louisville Negro parish, St. Augustine's, in 1866. Consecrated first Bishop of Peoria, Ill., 1877. "A great influence on US Catholic education." Died 1916 at Peoria.

L ebanon, Kentucky remembers two of its favorite sons: Bishop Martin John Spalding and his nephew, Bishop John Lancaster Spalding.

END PAGES

DOCUMENTS / 1861 ALMANAC

A STATISTICAL LOOK AT CATHOLICISM IN THE DIOCESE OF LOUISVILLE THE YEAR THAT THE CIVIL WAR BEGAN. SOURCE: THE METROPOLITAN CATHOLIC ALMANAC (BALTIMORE, JOHN MURPHY AND CO., 1861). THE EASTERN SECTION OF KENTUCKY HAD BEEN CONSTITUTED AS THE DIOCESE OF COVINGTON IN 1853. THE WESTERN SECTIONS ARE INCLUDED HERE. THAT PORTION OF KENTUCKY WOULD BECOME THE DIOCESE OF OWENSBORO IN 1937.

New Series, No. 3.

THE

METROPOLITAN

CATHOLIC ALMANAC,

AND

LAITY'S DIRECTORY,

FOR THE

United States, Canada, and the British Provinces.

1861.

BALTIMORE:

PRINTED AND PUBLISHED BY JOHN MURPHY & CO.
MARBLE BUILDING, 182 BALTIMORE STREET.

LONDON:...CATHOLIC PUBLISHING COMPANY.

Sold by all Catholic Booksellers.

DIOCESE OF LOUISVILLE.

ESTABLISHED 1808.

Comprises that part of Kentucky lying West of the Kentucky River and the Western limit of Carroll, Owen, Franklin, Woodford, Jessamine, Garrard, Rock Castle, Laurel and Whitley Counties.

DECEASED AND FORMER PRELATES.

Rt. Rev. BENEDICT JOSEPH FLAGET, D.D., consecrated Bishop of Bardstown, November 4, 1910; died in 1850.
Rt. Rev. JOHN B. DAVID, D.D., consecrated Bishop of Mauricastro, and Coadjutor of Bardstown, August 15, 1819; died in 1841.
Rt. Rev. GUY IGNATIUS CHABRAT, D.D., consecrated Bishop of Bolina, and Coadjutor of Bardstown, July 20, 1834; resigned in 1847.

PRESENT BISHOP.

Rt. Rev. MARTIN JOHN SPALDING, D.D., 2d Bishop, consecrated Sept. 10, 1848, Bishop of Lengone, and Coadjutor to the Bishop of Louisville.

VICARS GENERAL.

V. Rev. D. A. Deparcq.   V. Rev. B. J. Spalding, D.D.
V. Rev. F. Chambige, D.D.

COUNCIL OF THE BISHOP.

Very Rev. D. A. Deparcq, V. G.   Rev. J. B. Hutchins,
Very Rev. B. J. Spalding, D.D., V. G.   Rev. J. A. Bokel, O.S.D.
Very Rev. Francis Chambige, V. G.   Rev. Thos. O'Neill,
Rev. E. J. Durbin,   Rev. A. Degauquier,
Rev. James Elliott,   Rev. P. J. Lavialle,
Rev. W. S. Coomes,   Rev. M. M. Coghlan.

Chancellor and Secretary—Rev. J. H. Bekkers.
Consultors for Ecclesiastical Courts—Very Rev. F. Chambige and Rev. James Elliott.
Notary—Rev. E. O'Driscoll.

CHURCHES AND CLERGY.

Louisville, Jefferson Co., Cathedral of the Assumption.
Rt. Rev. Martin J. Spalding, D.D.
Very Rev. B. J. Spalding, D.D., Vic. Gen. and Rector; Rev. J. H. Bekkers, and Rev. H. Brady. There are three regular Masses on Sundays and Holydays at 6½, 8 and 10 A.M. in summer, and at 7, 8½, and 10½ A.M. in the winter; Sermons at 8 and 10 A.M. Masses; Vespers 3½ P.M. in Summer, and 3 P.M. in winter.
St. Boniface (German), Green street, residence adjoining; Rev. Edmund Etschmann, O.S.F., Rev. Dionysius Abarth, O.S.F. High Mass at 10 A. M. in summer, and 10½ A. M. in winter; Vespers at 2 and 2½ P.M.
Immaculate Conception (German), corner of 8th and Grayson streets, residence adjoining; Rev. F. X. Van Deutekom. High Mass at 10 and 10½ A.M.; Vespers 2½ and 3 P.M.
St. Martin's (German), Shelby street, residence adjoining; Rev. Leander Streber, O.S.F. and Rev. Anthony Muller, O.S.F. High Mass at 10 and 10½ A.M.; Vespers at 3 and 3½ P.M.
St. Patrick's Chapel, 13th street, residence adjoining; Rev. Thomas Joyce. High Mass at 9 and 9½ A. M.; Vespers at 3 P. M.
St. Peter's Church (German), 16th street, beyond Kentucky, attended by the Rev. Franciscan Fathers. High Mass at 9 and 9½ A. M.; Vespers at 3 P. M.
St. John's Church, Walnut and Clay sts.; Rev. L. Bax, and Rev. P. Fermont. High Mass at 10 and 10½ A. M.; Vespers 3 and 3½ P. M.

100   DIOCESE OF LOUISVILLE.

Chapel of the Seven Sorrows, 8th street, attached to the Convent of the Good Shepherd. Mass said daily by Rev. H. Brady, of the Cathedral.

Chapel of St. Aloysius, 4th street. Mass said occasionally by one of the clergy from the Cathedral.

Chapel of the Immaculate Conception, at St. Vincent's Orphan Asylum, Rev. W. S. Coomes.

Notre Dame du Port (Portland), Rev. J. J. Vital, who resides at the church, and is Chaplain of Cedar Grove Academy.

Bardstown, Nelson Co., St. Joseph's, Rev. Thos. O'Neill, S.J., Rev. Charles Truyens, and A. Levisse, S.J.

Bear Creek, Grayson Co., St. Augustine's, Rev. J. B. Vandemergel.

Bedford, Trimble Co., attended from Madison, Indiana.

Bell's Coal Mines, Crittenden Co., attended from the Sac. Heart, Union Co.

Belmont's Furnace, Bullit Co., Rev. Michael Bouchet.

Bethlehem Convent, Hardin Co., Immac. Conception, Rev. A. Degauquier, Chaplain and Director.

Bowling Green, Warren Co., new church, now occupied for Divine service. Rev. Jos. De Vries.

Big Run, Jefferson Co., St. Andrew's, attended by Rev. Franciscan Fathers.

Brandenburg, Meade Co., attended from Flint Island.

Clear Creek, Hardin Co., St. Clare's, Rev. C. J. Coomes.

Clifty, Grayson Co., St. Paul's, Rev. J. B. Van De Mergel.

Cloverport, Breckenridge Co., new brick church, Rev. Patrick Cassidy, once a month, from St. Lawrence's.

Dycusburg, Crittenden Co., Rev. E. J. Durbin.

Elizabethtown, Crittenden Co., St. James', Rev. A. Degauquier.

Eminence, Henry Co., new church building.

Fairfield, Nelson Co., St Michael's, Rev. Jas. Elliot.

Flint Island, Meade Co., St. Teresa's, Rev. Patrick McNicholas.

Franklin, Simpson Co., station, attended by Rev. Jos. De Vries.

Gethsemani, Nelson Co., residence of the Trappists. Mass every Sunday.

Hardinsburg, Breckenridge Co., St. Romuald's, Rev. Patrick Cassidy, once a month.

Hawesville, Hancock Co., Rev. P. Cassidy. New church building, and now used for service.

Henderson, Henderson Co., a new brick church under roof, and nearly ready for service. Attended once a month from S. Heart.

Hickman, Fulton Co., Rev. Martin Beyhurst, once a month. New church.

Hodgensville, La Rue Co., Our Lady of Mercy, Rev. F. De Meulder, and from St. Thomas', once a month.

Holy Cross, Marion Co., Holy Cross, Rev. Francis Wuyts.

Holy Mary's, Marion Co., Holy Mary, Very Rev. D. A. Duparcq, Rev. A. A. Aud.

Kelly's Furnace, Caldwell Co., station, attended by Rev. E. J. Durbin.

Lebanon, Marion Co., St. Augustine's, Rev. J. B. Hutchins.

Lewis Bottom, Hancock Co., St. Columba's, Rev. Patrick Cassidy, once a month.

Long Lick, Breckenridge Co., St. Anthony's, Rev. J. B. Vandemergel, once a month.

Loretto Convent, Marion Co., Seven Sorrows, Rev. Francis Wuyts.

Madisonville, Hopkins Co., station, attended by Rev. E. J. Durbin.

Manton, Washington Co., Holy Rosary, attended from St. Rose.

Milton, Trimble Co., station, attended from Madison, Indiana.

Morganfield, Union Co., attended from the Sacred Heart.

Mount Merino, Breckenridge Co., Guardian Angels, Rev. P. Nicholas, once a month.

Mount Washington, Bullit Co., St. F. Xavier's, Rev. Michael Bouchet.

DIOCESE OF LOUISVILLE.   101

Nazareth Convent, Nelson Co., St. Vincent of Paul's, Rev. Jos. Haseltine.

New Haven, Nelson Co., St. Catherine's, Rev. Francis De Meulder.

Nolin, Grayson Co., St. Benedict's, Rev. J. B. Vandemergel, once a month.

Owensboro', Daviess Co., St. Stephen's, Rev. Eugene O'Callaghan, three times a month. New brick church, completed.

Paducan, McCracken Co., St. F. de Sales, Rev. Michael Power, who also attends Smithland, and other adjoining Missions.

Panther Greek, Daviess Co., St. Alphonsus, Rev. Polydore Fermont, Rev. Michael Power.

Raywick, Marion Co., St. F. Xavier's, Rev. James Quinn.

Red Mills, Larue Co., st'n, attended by Franciscan Fathers from Louisville.

Sacred Heart of Jesus, Union Co., Sacred Heart, Rev. E. J. Durbin, Rev. William Bourke.

St. Ambrose, Union Co., St. Ambrose, attended from the Sacred Heart.

St. John Chrysostom's, new church, Adair Co., Rev. J. B. Hutchins, once a month.

St. Catherine of Sienna's Chapel, Washington Co., attended from St. Rose.

St. Charles, Marion Co., attended by Rev. Peter De Frime.

St. Francis of Sales, Taylor Co., attended by Rev. J. B. Hutchins.

St. Gregory's, Deatsville, Nelson Co., attended by Rev. Michael Bouchet.

St. Jerome's, Graves Co., Rev. Martin Beyhurst. (P. O. Fancy Farm.)

St. Ignatius, Hardin Co., station, attended by Rev. A. Degauquier, once a month. (P. O. Elizabethtown.)

St. John the Baptist's, Hardin Co., station, attended by Rev. A. Degauquier, once a month.

St. John the Baptist, Bullit Co., station, attended by Rev. Mich'l Bouchet.

St. John the Evangelist, McCracken Co., station, attended by Rev. Michael Power, twice a month.

St. Lawrence, Daviess Co., brick church, attended by Rev. M. M. Coghland, and Rev. Patrick Cassidy.

St. Martin's, Meade Co., frame church, attended by Rev. C. J. Coomes. (P. O. Garnettsville.)

St. Mary of the Woods, Daviess Co., attended by Rev. Patrick Cassidy.

St. Patrick's, Meade's Co., attended by Rev. C. J. Coomes. The Rev. R. A. Abell resides near this church, having retired from active service on account of age and infirmities.

St. Rose's, Washington Co., attended by the Dominican Fathers. Mass every Sunday and Holyday. A fine new church of stone, completed.

St. Raphael's, Panther Creek, Daviess Co., Rev. Eugene O'Callaghan. Church has been burned down, but will soon be rebuilt.

St. Thomas, Nelson Co., Rev. Edmund O'Driscoll.

St. Vincent, Nelson Co., Rev. Francis Wuyts. A neat brick church has been built.

St. Anthony, Long Lick, attended by Rev. J. B. Vandemergel, once a month.

Shepherdsville, Bullit Co., station, attended occasionally by Rev. T. Joyce.

Shelbyville, Shelby Co., new church building.

Springfield, Washington Co., St. Dominic's, attended from St. Rose. A new church has been erected at Thompsonville, a few miles north of Springfield.

Summerville, Green Co., station, attended by Rev. J. B. Hutchins.

Sunfish Creek, Edmundson Co., St. J. the Evangelist, Rev. J. B. Vandemergel, once a month.

Taylorsville, Spencer Co., All Saints, Rev. James Elliott.

Thompsonville, Church of the Assumption, attended twice a month from St. Rose.

Uniontown, Union Co., a new church has been nearly completed, Rev. E. J. Durbin.

102   DIOCESE OF LOUISVILLE.

LITERARY AND RELIGIOUS INSTITUTIONS.

St. Thomas' Preparatory Seminary, near Bardstown, Rev. Francis Chambige, Superior; Rev. E. O'Driscol, Rev. M. Chazal, Rev. J. F. Reed. (P. O. Bardstown.) Number of pupils 60.

Abbey of Our Lady of Latrappe, New Haven, Nelson Co., Rev. B. M. Benedict, O. C., Superior. There are in this community 64 members, 18 of whom, including eleven priests, belong to the choir, the remainder are lay-brothers or novices.

Dominican Convent of St. Rose, near Springfield, Rev. J. A. Bokel, O.P., Prior; Very Rev. T. A. O'Brien, Ex Pro., O.P.; Rev. J. V. Daly, O.P., Supervisor; Rev. C. D. Bowling, O.P., Conf. Mon.; Rev. J. T. Ryan, O.P.; Rev. P. V. Keogh, O.P., Procurator; Rev. P. Turner, O.P.; Rev. J. Meagher, O.P., Novice Master; Rev. A. Rooney, O.P. There are 11 Professed Novices in the Convent, and 3 in Rome, at St. Sabina's, to finish their studies. Lay brothers 10. Missions attended from St. Rose—Manton, Springfield. Harrodsburg, Thompsonville, besides several stations.

St Joseph's College, Bardstown, Rev. Thos. O'Neil, S.J., President, Rev. John S. Verdir, S. J., Vice President; Rev. Francis P. O'Loghlen, S. J., Rev. Joseph A. Fastré, S. J., Rev. Theodore De Leeuw, S. J., Rev. James Hayes, S. J., Rev. James Halpin, S. J., Rev. Anthony Levisse, S. J., Rev. Francis X. Wippern, S. J. Number of boarders 168.

St. Mary's College, Lebanon, Marion Co., Rev. P. J. Lavialle, President, Rev. Jos. Elder, Vice-President. 125 boarders.

Brothers of the Christian Instruction of the Sacred Hearts of Jesus and Mary, from Puy, France; they are five in number, and reside at the Cathedral parochial school of St. Aloysius, Fourth street, where they conduct a Free Parochial School, and a Select School. Number of boys about 200. Brother Florimond, Superior.

House of the Xaverien Brothers, Green street, No. 524, Louisville, Ky., Brother Paul, Superior. Brothers in the community 10. They direct the following schools:—St. Patrick's school, (English), pupils 200; St. John's, (English), pupils 240; St. Boniface, (German), pupils 300; School of the Immaculate Conception, (German), pupils 200. There are also parochial schools attached to St. Martin's church, (German), taught by the Ursuline Sisters, and a Franciscan Brother.

Mother House and Academy of the Sisters of Charity of Nazareth, near Bardstown. Mother Frances Gardiner, Sup'r. Religious 50, boarders 240.

The Sisters also conduct the following:—

1. *Presentation Female Academy*, Louisville, 129 pupils. Sister Frances Xavia Sister-servant.

2. *St. Frances' Female Academy*, Owensboro', 75 pupils. Sister Constantia Robinson, Sister-servant.

3. *St. Vincent's Female Academy*, Morganfield, 100 pupils. Sister Elizabeth Suttle, Sister-servant.

4. *Bethlehem Day School*, Bardstown, 45 pupils. Sister Alice Drury, Sister-servant.   [servant.

5. *Cathedral Free School*, Louisville, 180 pupils. Sister Baptista, Sister-
6. *St. Patrick's Free School*, Louisville, 150 pupils. Sister Rosalie Huff, Sister-servant.

7. *Free School at the Asylum*, Louisville, 150 pupils. Sister Julia Hobbs, Sister-servant.

Notre Dame du Port, Free School, at Portland, attended by the Sisters of Cedar Grove Academy. 60 pupils.

Sisters of Loretto, Mother House and Academy, Marion Co. Mother Berlindes Downs, Mother Superior of the Society. Sisters 40, pupils 50.

The Sisters of Loretto have also—

1. *Convent and Academy of Culvary*, near Lebanon, Sister Clotilda Gravis, Superior. Sisters 18, pupils 70.

2. *Bethlehem Convent and Academy*, near Elizabethtown, Hardin Co., Sister Bertha Bowls, Superior. Sisters 15, pupils 70.

     DIOCESE OF LOUISVILLE.   103

3. *Cedar Grove Convent and Academy*, Portland, Ky., about 75 boarders. Sister Eliz. Hayden, Superior. Sisters 15, pupils 50.

Dominican Convent and Academy of St. Catharine of Sienna, Washington Co. (P. O. Springfield). Mother Mary Magdalene, Superior. Religious 20, pupils 120.

Sisters of Our Lady of Charity of the Good Shepherd, on Eighth street. This is the Provincial House for a large portion of the United States. They have erected a large new building during the last year. Mother Mary Ignatia Ward, Provincial.

Ursuline Convent and Academy, Louisville, Mother Salesia Reitmeier, Superior; Professed 6; Novices 5; Pupils 20; Day School 30.

The School of the Congregation, St. Martin, is directed by these Sisters. Number of scholars 250.

School Sisters of Notre Dame, reside at St. Boniface, Green street, and attend the large parochial school, for girls, attached. They are three in number.

ASYLUMS, &c.

Convent of the Sisters of Our Lady of Charity of the Good Shepherd, Louisville, Mother M. Ignatius Ward, Provincial and Superior. Religious 25, Magdalenes 20, Penitents 45.

St. Thomas' Male Orphan Asylum, near Bardstown, Brother Joseph and Brother Lawrence, Teachers. Number of orphans 80.

St. Joseph's Male Orphan Asylam (German), Louisville. directed by the Reverend German Clergymen of the city. Number of orphans 25. The Board of Trustees have lately purchased a new house for this Asylum, on the corner of Green and Preston streets.

St. Vincent Female Orphan Asylum, Louisville, 140 orphans, under the Sisters of Charity. Sister Julia Hobbs, Sister-servant.

St. Joseph's Infirmary, Louisville, under the Sisters of Charity, 15 to 30 patients. Sister Mary Agnes McDermott, Sister-servant. Eight Sisters, average number of patients 25.

In Louisville there are three Conferences of St. Vincent de Paul, established at the Cathedral and at the chapels of St. John the Evangelist and St. Patrick. The members labor with great zeal and are doing much good. B. J. Webb, Esq., is the President of the Society.

There are also in the city various other charitable societies of both men and women organized in the different churches, under the direction of the Reverend Clergy.

The Sodalities for young men and for young women, as well as for boys and girls, at the Cathedral, are in a highly flourishing condition, and they afford much edification. There are similar Sodalities at St. Patrick's.

There is likewise in the Cathedral congregation, with the approbation of the Bishop, a Catholic Institute for promoting library culture among young men.

There are also Parochial Schools for boys and girls established in all the Congregations of the city, in which about *two thousand five hundred children* receive the benefits of a sound Christian education.

RECAPITULATION.

Priests of Religious Orders	35	Male Religious Institutions	4
Secular Priests	48	Female Religious Institutions	5
Priests engaged in Missions	56	Preparatory Seminary	1
Priests otherwise engaged	27	Colleges	2
Churches	72	Academies for Young Ladies	16
Churches building	5	Male Free Schools in Louisville	7
Stations, about	100	Female " "	3
Ecclesiastical Institutions	1	Baptisms (for one year) about	3,000
Clerical Students	20	Catholic Population, about	65,000

A GUIDE TO BEHAVIOR IN CHURCH C.1915 FROM A SMALL PUBLICATION OF ST. JOSEPH CHURCH, LOUISVILLE — AND SOME ACCOMPANYING ADVERTISMENTS.

IT IS THE CORRECT THING.

To make one's Easter duty.

To always be in time for Mass and other services of the church.

To take Holy Water on entering the church.

To make the sign of the cross on the person and not in the air.

To genuflect on the right knee, and have it touch the floor.

To remember that the king of kings is present on the Altar, and conduct yourself accordingly.

To avoid whispering, laughing and looking about in Church.

To walk gently up the aisle, if one is unavoidably detained after the services have begun.

To make a short act of adoration on bended knees after entering the pew.

To be devout and collected at the different parts of the Mass.

To remember that bodily presence in the Church, with the mind wandering on temporal concerns, does not fulfill the precept of hearing Mass.

To pay attention to the sermon, and make it the subject of your thoughts during the day, as also during the week.

To remember when special collections are to be taken up to have your contribution ready in your hand.

To make a practice of putting something in the offertory contribution box every Sunday. This should never be omitted at Holy Mass. This collection is of apostolic origin.

To train children in this practice.

To listen to the music as a means of elevating the heart to God.

For a gentleman occupying a pew to move in or to rise and let ladies pass in before him.

For pew holders to offer seats in their pews to strangers.

For men too stingy to have a seat of their own in Church, to occupy the free pews, and not blockade the entrance by standing, or kneeling on one knee, around it.

To avoid coughing, moving the feet around, or making any noise to the annoyance of the clergy and people.

To be punctilious in following the ceremonies of the Church, standing, kneeling, etc., at the proper times.

For non-Catholics who go to Catholic Churches to conform to the services and to remember that this is the requirement of good breeding.

For members of the choir to sing for the glory of God, and not for their own.

To take an earnest Protestant to hear a good sermon.

To remain kneeling until the last prayers have been said and the Priest has retired to the Sacristy.

IT IS NOT THE CORRECT THING.

To be late for Mass or any Church service.

To stalk hurriedly and noisily up the aisle.

To ignore the Holy Water font at the entrance.

To make the sign of the cross as if fanning the flies.

To give a little bobbing courtesy instead of the proper genuflections before entering one's pew.

To whisper, cough or cause distraction to those around.

To go to sleep or read the prayer book during the sermon. This is unpardonable

To deliberately turn around, stare up at the choir, or at those entering the Church.

To be in an ecstatic condition of devotion when the contribution box approaches.

To forget all about the special collections for the Church Debt, etc.

To go to High Mass simply to listen to the music, as one would go to the opera.

For the person occupying the end seat to scowl forbiddingly at those who seek to enter the pew.

For a person to go into a private pew without an invitation.

To make a rush for the door before the Priest has descended the Altar to begin the concluding prayers.

To go to church the last moment and leave it the first.

To kneel on only one knee, or to emulate the position of the bear when saying one's prayers.

For members of the choir to forget that the choir loft is part of the Church, and that talking, laughing, giggling, chewing gum and other practices have been known to prevail in some choirs, are strictly out of place. It has been remarked that in choir conduct Catholic members, to their shame, suffer in comparison with Protestants.

SELECT BIBLIOGRAPHY

Diane Aprile. **The Abbey of Gethsemani: Place of Peace and Paradox** (Louisville 1998).

Joseph Angela Boone OSU (ed.) **The Roman Catholic Diocese of Owensboro, Kentucky** (Owensboro 1995).

Thomas D. Clark. **A History of Kentucky** (Lexington 1977).

Clyde F. Crews. **An American Holy Land** (Wilmington 1987).

Mary Frederica Dudine, OSB. **The Castle on the Hill** (Ferdinand, Indiana 1967).

Judy Hayden (ed.) **This Far By Faith: The Story of Catholicity in Western Kentucky** (Owensboro 1987).

Lowell Harrison and James Klotter. **A New History of Kentucky** (Lexington 1997).

Albert Kleber OSB. **A History of St. Meinrad Archabbey** (St. Meinrad 1954).

John Kleber (ed.) **The Kentucky Encyclopedia** (Lexington 1992).

John Kleber (ed.) **The Encyclopedia of Louisville** (Lexington 2000).

Agnes Geraldine McGann SCN. **Nativism in Kentucky to 1860** (Washington 1944).

Mary Ramona Mattingly SCN. **The Catholic Church on the Kentucky Frontier 1785-1812** (Washington 1936).

Paul E. Ryan. **History of the Diocese of Covington, Kentucky** (Covington 1954).

J. H. Schauinger. **Cathedrals in the Wilderness** (Milwaukee 1952).

M. Carol Schroeder. **The Catholic Church in the Diocese of Vincennes 1847-1877** (Washington 1946).

Martin John Spalding. **Sketches of the Early Catholic Missions of Kentucky** (Louisville 1844).

Robert M. Taylor, Jr. et. al. **Indiana: A New Historical Guide** (Indianapolis 1989).

Benedict Webb. **The Centenary of Catholicity in Kentucky** (Louisville 1884).

Joseph M. White. **Where God's People Meet: A Guide to Significant Religious Places in Indiana** (Carmel, Indiana 1996).

Monks of Gethsemani Abbey at a service
outside Our Lady of the Woods Chapel,
Bellarmine University. December, 2001.

PHOTOGRAPHIC SOURCES

In addition to the photographers and others earlier listed in Acknowledgments (p.9), the author additionally wishes to thank the following for their kind assistance in providing pictures or information:

Mrs. Kenneth Barker

Sr. Mary Quentin Barth *(Sisters of Mercy of Louisville)*

Fr. Noah Casey *(St. Meinrad Archabbey)*

Mr. Basil Doerhoefer and Family

Mr. Joseph Duerr *(**The Record**)*

Ms. Claudia Fitch *(Louisville Free Public Library)*

Sr. Mary Rose Paula Foltz *(Sisters of Notre Dame of Covington)*

Dr. John Gatton *(Bellarmine University)*

Ms. Jane Guentert *(Diocese of Lexington)*

Mr. Art Jester *(**Lexington Herald-Leader**)*

Ms. Marsha Kohl *(Cathedral of the Assumption, Louisville)*

Ms. Lois Martin *(Daughters of Charity, Mater Dei Provincialate, Evansville)*

Ms. Aggie Noonan *(Presentation Academy)*

Sr. Mary Prisca Pfeffer *(Sisters of Mercy of Louisville)*

Fr. Joseph Rautenberg, Ph.D. *(Archdiocese of Indianapolis)*

Mr. John Spugnardi *(Bellarmine University)*

Sr. Fidelis Tracy *(Congregation of the Sisters of Divine Providence, Melbourne, Ky.)*

Sr. Theresa Volking *(Benedictine Sisters of St. Walburg Monastery)*

Ms. Angela Wiggins *(Cathedral of the Assumption, Louisville)*

Abbreviations used below:

AAL – Archives of the Archdiocese of Louisville, CFC – Clyde F. Crews

❖❖❖

Front Cover: At The Abbey Of Gethsemani, © Dan Dry

Back Cover: Louisville Cathedral, CFC; *(inset photo)* Provided by Thomas D. Clark

End Flap: Author's Photo, © Patrick L. Pfister

❖❖❖

Frontispiece: Bellarmine Chapel, photo by David Hockensmith

❖❖❖

Page 7	Provided by Dr. Thomas D. Clark	*Page 27*	CFC
Page 8	Collection of the Speed Art Museum, Louisville, Kentucky.	*Page 28*	CFC
		Page 29	CFC
Page 10	© Patrick L. Pfister	*Page 30*	CFC
Page 14	© John Nation	*Page 33*	CFC
Page 16	CFC	*Page 34*	AAL; CFC *(inset)*
Page 17	© Patrick L. Pfister; CFC *(right inset)*	*Page 35*	Joe Duerr, **The Record**, Louisville
Page 18	CFC	*Page 36*	AAL; CFC *(inset)*
Page 19	CFC	*Page 37*	© Patrick L. Pfister; AAL *(c.1900 inset)*
Page 20	CFC	*Page 38*	CFC *(left side)*; AAL *(right side)*; © Patrick L. Pfister *(bottom 2 insets, right)*
Page 21	CFC; © Patrick L. Pfister *(insets)*		
Page 22	AAL; CFC *(bottom left, tomb inset)*; Cathedral of the Assumption Records		
		Page 39	AAL; © Patrick L. Pfister *(inset)*
Page 23	Archives of the Nazareth Motherhouse *(Catherine Spalding)*	*Page 40*	AAL; © John Nation *(inset)*
		Page 41	© Patrick L. Pfister; CFC *(end right inset of school)*
Page 24	CFC; © Dan Dry *(inset)*		
Page 25	© Dan Dry	*Page 43*	CFC
Page 26	**The Messenger**, Evansville; CFC *(inset)*	*Page 44*	AAL

Page 45 © Patrick L. Pfister *(2 left side)*; AAL *(bottom right inset)*; CFC *(center insets and right)*

Page 46 AAL; CFC *(bottom inset)*

Page 47 AAL; CFC *(bottom inset)*

Page 48 CFC

Page 49 CFC

Page 50 CFC

Page 51 CFC

Page 52 CFC; AAL *(inset)*

Page 53 AAL

Page 54 CFC; AAL *(right inset)*

Page 55 © Patrick L. Pfister

Page 56 AAL

Page 57 AAL

Page 58 CFC

Page 59 CFC

Page 61 CFC

Page 62 AAL

Page 63 CFC

Page 64 CFC

Page 65 CFC

Page 66 AAL

Page 67 CFC

Page 69 CFC

Page 70 AAL; CFC *(inset)*

Page 71 AAL

Page 72 AAL

Page 73 AAL

Page 74 CFC

Page 75 CFC

Page 76 CFC

Page 77 CFC

Page 79 CFC

Page 80 CFC

Page 81 AAL

Page 82 CFC

Page 83 CFC

Page 84 CFC

Page 85 CFC

Page 86 Archives of the Diocese of Owensboro; CFC *(bottom)*

Page 87 CFC

Page 88 CFC

Page 89 CFC

Page 90 CFC

Page 91 CFC

Page 92 CFC

Page 93 CFC

Page 95 CFC

Page 96 CFC

Page 97 CFC

Page 98 CFC

Page 99 CFC

Page 100 CFC

Page 101 CFC

Pages 102-103 CFC

Page 104 CFC

Page 105 CFC

Page 106 CFC

Page 107 CFC

Page 108 CFC

Page 109 CFC

Page 110 CFC

Page 111 CFC

Page 112 © Patrick L. Pfister

Page 115 Archives of St. Meinrad Archabbey; CFC *(bottom)*

Pages 116-117 CFC

Page 118 Archives of St. Meinrad Archabbey; CFC *(bottom)*

Page 119 CFC

Page 120 CFC

Page 121 CFC

Pages 122-123 © Patrick L. Pfister

Page 123 CFC *(bottom inset)*

Page 124 © Patrick L. Pfister; Archives of Gethsemani Abbey *(top inset)*; CFC *(historical marker insets)*

Page 125 Archives of Gethsemani Abbey

Page 127 CFC

Page 128 Archives of the Loretto Motherhouse

Page 129 Archives of the Loretto Motherhouse

Page 130 CFC

Page 131 CFC; © John Nation *(crucifix at bottom center)*

Pages 132-133 CFC

Page 133 CFC; Archives of the Nazareth Motherhouse *(bottom right inset)*

Page 134 CFC; Archives of the Nazareth Motherhouse *(bottom 2 right insets)*

Page 135 Archives of the Nazareth Motherhouse; © Patrick L. Pfister *(bottom left inset)*

Page 136 Archives of the Nazareth Motherhouse

Page 137 Archives of the Nazareth Motherhouse

Pages 138-139 CFC

Page 140 CFC

Page 141 Archives of the Dominican Sisters, Springfield

Page 142 Archives of the Dominican Sisters, Springfield

Page 143 Archives of the Dominican Sisters, Springfield

Page 144 AAL; CFC *(bottom insets)*

Page 145 Archives of the Ursuline Sisters, Louisville; CFC *(inset)*

Page 146 Archives of the Ursuline Sisters, Louisville

Page 147 Archives of the Ursuline Sisters, Louisville

Page 148 CFC

Page 149 Archives of the Ursuline Sisters, Maple Mount; CFC *(bottom insets)*

Page 150 Archives of the Ursuline Sisters, Maple Mount

Page 151 Archives of the Ursuline Sisters, Maple Mount

Page 152 CFC

Page 153 CFC; Archives of the Sisters of Divine Providence *(bottom right inset)*

Page 154 CFC

Page 155 CFC; Archives of St. Walburg Monastery (bottom right inset)

Page 157 CFC

Page 158 CFC

Page 159 CFC

Page 160 CFC

Page 161 CFC

Page 162 CFC

Page 163 Archives of the Sisters of Providence

Page 164 CFC

Page 165 CFC

Page 166 CFC

Page 167 The Mater Dei photo *(taken by Barbara Paul)* and the Elizabeth Seton photo are used by permission of the Archives, Daughters of Charity, Mater Dei Provincialate; CFC *(other photos)*

Page 168 CFC

Page 171 CFC

Page 172 CFC; Doerhoefer Family Collection *(inset)*

Page 173 CFC

Page 174 CFC

Page 175 CFC; Doyle Family Collection *(bottom right inset)*

Page 176 CFC

Page 177 CFC

Page 178 CFC

Page 179 CFC

Page 180 CFC

Page 181 CFC

Page 182 CFC

Page 183 CFC

Page 185 CFC

Page 186 CFC

Page 187 CFC

Page 188 CFC

Page 189 CFC; Archives of the Loretto Motherhouse (Connor inset)

Page 191 CFC

Page 192 CFC

Page 193 CFC

Page 194 CFC

Page 195 CFC

Page 197 CFC

Page 198 CFC

Page 199 CFC

Page 200 CFC

Page 201 CFC; Archives of the Archdiocese of Indianapolis (bottom right)

Page 202 © Dan Dry

Page 204 CFC

Page 205 CFC

Page 206 CFC

Page 207 CFC

Page 208 CFC

Page 209 Collection of Owensboro Museum of Fine Art, Owensboro, Kentucky

Page 210 CFC

Page 211 CFC

Page 212 CFC

Page 213 CFC

Page 214 CFC

Page 215 CFC

Page 216 CFC

Page 217 CFC

Page 218 Collection of The Speed Art Museum, Louisville, Kentucky

Page 220 CFC

Page 221 CFC

Page 222 CFC

Page 223 Collection of The Speed Art Museum, Louisville, Kentucky

Page 224 Collection of The Speed Art Museum, Louisville, Kentucky

Page 225 CFC

Page 226 AAL

Page 227 CFC

Page 228 CFC

Page 229 CFC

Page 230 CFC

Page 231 CFC; AAL (bottom)

Page 232 Family Collection of Mrs. Joyce Alagia *(Graduation Photo)*; CFC

Page 233 CFC

Page 234 CFC

Page 235 CFC

Page 236 CFC

Page 237 Family Collection of Mrs. Joyce Alagia; AAL *(bottom)*

Page 238 AAL

Page 239 AAL

Page 240 AAL

Page 241 Archives of the Sisters of Mercy of Louisville; AAL

Page 242 AAL

Page 243 AAL; CFC *(McAuley)*; Private Collection of CFC *(First Communicant and Two Sisters)*.

Page 244 CFC

Page 245 CFC

Pages 246-248 CFC Collection

Page 249 AAL

Page 250 CFC

Page 252 From respective diocesan directories.

THE ARCHDIOCESE OF LOUISVILLE

The Archdiocese of Louisville was established at Bardstown in 1808 and moved to Louisville in 1841. It was named an archdiocese in 1937.

THE ARCHDIOCESE OF INDIANAPOLIS

The Archdiocese of Indianapolis was established at Vincennes in 1834 and moved to Indianapolis in 1898. It was named an archdiocese in 1944.

THE DIOCESE OF COVINGTON

The Diocese of Covington was established in 1853.

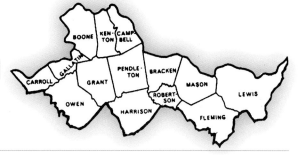

THE DIOCESE OF OWENSBORO

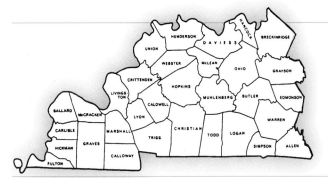

The Diocese of Owensboro was established in 1937.

THE DIOCESE OF EVANSVILLE

The Diocese of Evansville was established in 1944.

THE DIOCESE OF LEXINGTON

The Diocese of Lexington was established in 1988.

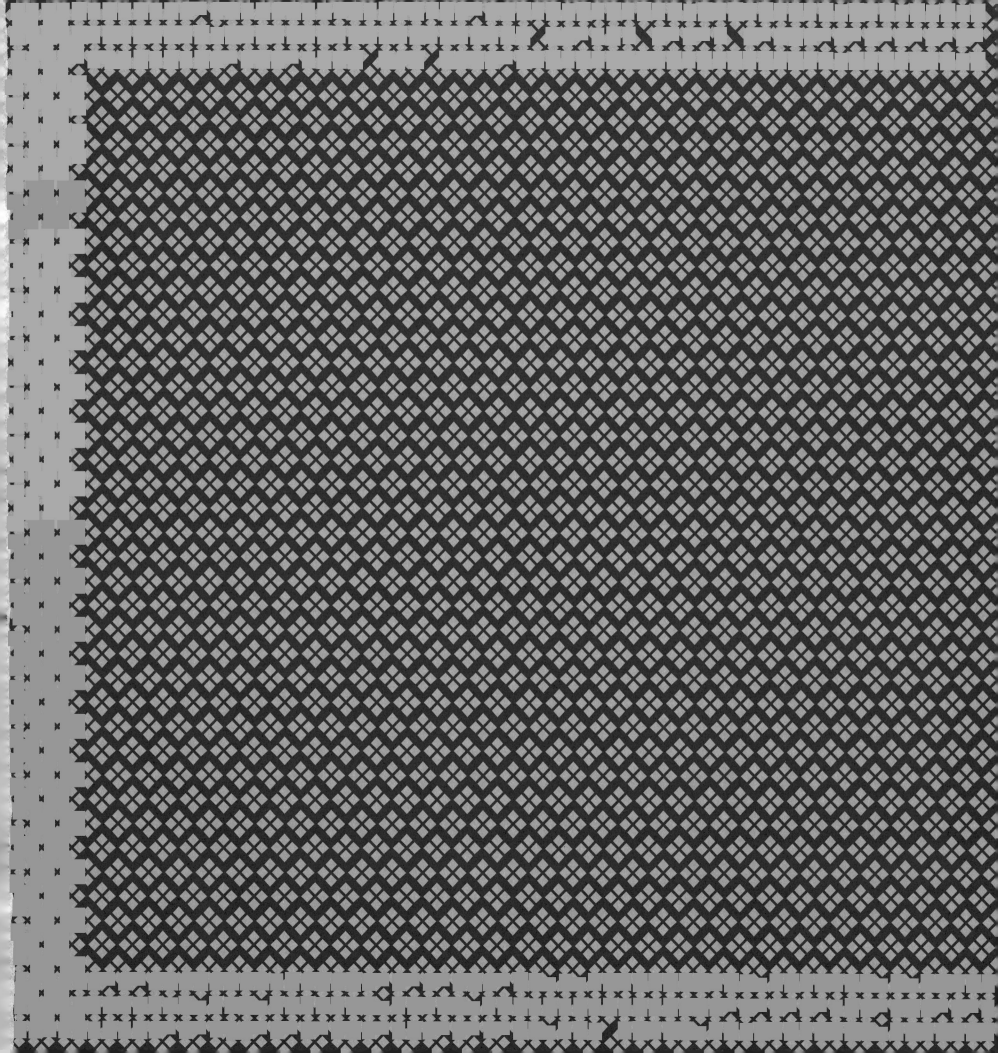